PUB WALKS IN THE NEW FOREST

DIANA SMITH

Ensign
PUBLICATIONS

First published in 1990 by
Ensign Publications
A division of Hampshire Books Ltd
2 Redcar Street
Southampton SO1 5LL

Reprinted 1990 (Twice) 1991 (With corrections)

ISBN 1 85455 058 6

Edited by David Graves
Cover design by The Design Laboratory
Maps by Sylvie Guttridge
Photograph by John Blay
Typeset by PageMerger, Southampton
Printed and bound in the UK by Conifer Press

INTRODUCTION

Routes

All of these walks keep to well defined tracks or footpaths as much as possible. In most cases the main route is about 6-7 km. (4 miles), about 2 hours at strolling pace, with shorter options indicated. Some of the routes overlap or can be linked to make a longer walk of 9 to 13 km. (6 to 8 miles). The distance and possible links are shown at the beginning of the notes for each walk and indicated on the maps.

Footwear

Many areas of the New Forest are low lying or marshy: * indicates a ford or especially muddy patches en route and suggests the need for wellies or boots, especially in winter or after wet weather.

Maps

For each walk there is a sketch map showing the main routes, special features, pubs and public car parks. It is advisable to carry a more detailed map with you, such as the Ordnance Survey 1:25,000 Outdoor Leisure Map of the New Forest. When walking in unfamiliar forest, it is often useful to also carry a compass to maintain a sense of direction or orientate the map.

Map Symbols : PH = Pub, P = Car Park, T = Toilets, D = Deer observation platform, + = Church or chapel, △ = campsite.

Pubs (Index page 90)

Each pub's address, phone number and map grid reference are supplied. The details of opening times, facilities and availability of food at each of the 50 pubs have been supplied by the publicans but are subject to change. Abbreviations are used as follows: P = Parking, G = Beer Garden, FR = Family Room.

The New Forest

The map on page 6 shows that the majority of the pubs (and thus starting points) are either around the edge of the Forest or clustered in the large villages of Lyndhurst and Brockenhurst. We can therefore explore the area from all directions, discover its secrets and experience the many facets of its character that make the New Forest unique.

Everywhere on these walks you are likely to encounter Commoners' animals grazing the heath or woodland – cows, ponies and donkeys, also pigs in late autumn. When William I declared this area part of his new hunting forest, the local peasants were no longer allowed to fence any land for fear of it impeding the deer. However, their domestic animals were allowed to graze by common right, hence the name "commoner".

Please remember that the New Forest is a source of valuable timber, a grazing place for stock and home to many rare native plants and animals. It is especially important to observe the Country Code and ensure that we leave no trace of our visit.

Pub Walks in the New Forest

- - - - - - **New Forest boundary**

o **Starting point of walk**

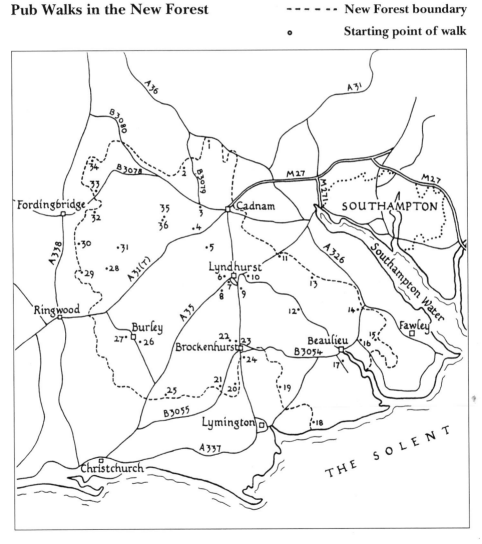

CONTENTS

Walk 1

Pub 1. **The Shoe Inn**,
Salisbury Road,
Plaitford, Hants.
Tel. Romsey (0794) 22397.

GR 276194   *11-3, 6-11*

P (both sides of main road) **G FR** Play Area
B&B very close.
Facilities for camping and caravans.
Snacks and full meals 12-2, 7-9.30.

Once a coaching house, it has real open fires. The original part of the pub was built in 1550. The thatched front was built 1711. Florence Nightingale tended soldiers at the inn (She is buried at Wellow Church). The last highwayman of the New Forest was caught at the inn and hung on Plaitford Common. There is a friendly female ghost in the main part of the bar.

Pub 2. **The Red Rover**
West Wellow, Romsey.
Tel. Romsey (0794) 22266.

GR 288192   *Mon.-Sat. 11-3, 6.30-11;*
Sun. 12-3, 7-10.30.

P G Dogs welcome on leads.
Snacks and full meals 12-2.15, 7-9.30.
Book 24 hours in advance for large parties.

Pub 3. **Rockingham Arms**
Canada Road,
West Wellow, Romsey.
Tel. Romsey (0794) 22473.

GR 289179   *Mon.-Fri. 11.45-3, 6-11;*
Sat. 11.15-3, 6-11;
Sun. 12-3, 7-10.30.

P G Play Area. Dogs welcome in bar
Barbecue area.
Snacks and full meals 12-3, 7-10.
Booking advised for restaurant.

A pub since the turn of the century. Real fire in the Forest Bar. Haunted well in garden. Access to the Forest.

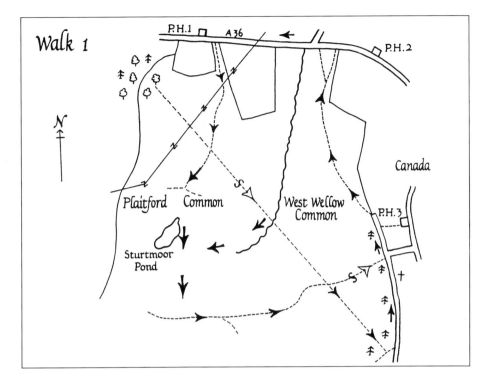

Walk 1.   PLAITFORD COMMON
5 or 6.5 km (3 or 4 miles.)

From The Shoe Inn, cross the road and a short way to the left is a stile. Beyond that a path through a wide grassy corridor between fields leads out to rolling open heath, dotted with gorse bushes.

Plaitford Common occupies the western two thirds of this area. It is one of five commons that form the Bramshaw Commons group and was given to the National Trust in two parts in 1928 and 1930. Although only included in the New Forest in 1964, it shares many of the characteristics: the open heath is maintained by the grazing of commoners' animals and is a valuable habitat for bog plants and lichens in particular and birds of open moors such as stonechat and nightjar. Sturtmoor Pond provides a breeding site for many dragonflies and damselflies and the whole area is designated a Site of Special Scientific Interest.

Your path heads slightly to the right, uphill, passing a marshy area on the right before going under the pylon line. Keep on until you reach the top of a low ridge.

9

From here there are panoramic views in all directions. To the north you may spot the mast on Dean Hill, 5 miles away.

A long track leads straight across the broad valley and beyond. This makes an easy route to follow, or you could add a short detour and visit Sturtmoor Pond. There are two ways to find the pond; either take the straight track down to its lowest point where heather gives way to grass near a tiny stream, then follow the ribbon of grass for about 400m up onto a small rise. From there you will see the pond slightly to your right. Alternatively, from the view point, go a little further west until the path starts to go downhill, then turn left and make your own way downhill through the heather. The pond is only 250m away. From the pond, head south, up the slopes of heather onto a ridge where you will find a broad sandy track running east-west.

Head east and as the track drops down slope a little, you will come to its junction with the long straight track. Go straight ahead towards the houses and chapel of Canada for a short walk. You may extend it by half a mile or so by following the rest of the straight track south eastwards to the far corner of Canada Common; then turn left and follow the road back up to the chapel.

A path, for the use of patrons, links the Rockingham Arms directly to this route. Follow the road north and continue uphill where the road ends. The path crosses a shallow valley and on the next rise you will pass a bench before descending to the A36.

Walk 2

Lamb Inn
Nomansland, Near Romsey.
Tel. Romsey (0794) 390246.

GR 253173   *11-3, 6-11.*

P Dogs welcome.
Snacks and full meals 12-2, 7-9.

*In the past there was uncertainty over boundaries.
Did this bit belong to Wiltshire, Hampshire, the Crown, or the Bishop of Winchester? Such a
situation attracted squatters who then claimed their own rights to land. The village was agreed
to be just outside the New Forest boundary and the county boundary runs through it. The pub
is in Wiltshire. Beside the pub are licensed tea rooms.*

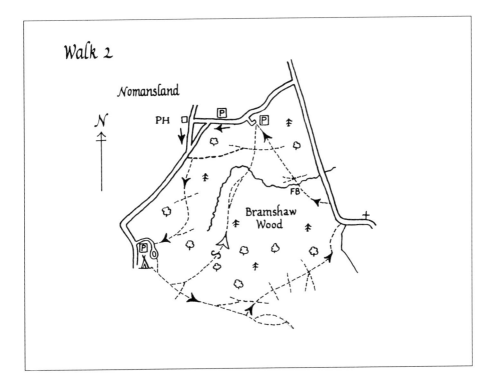

Walk 2.   ANCIENT AND ORNAMENTAL WOODLAND
3 or 5 km (2 or 3 miles.)

From the car park opposite the pub and from the top of the hill near Pipers Wait Car Park, you can see for miles to the north. Two large buildings in the distance are Melchett Court School and Landford Manor where Lord Nelson lived.

The first oak woodland that you pass is notable for the regularity of tree size, a sure sign that this was planted. The New Forest was an important source of timber for ships until the invention of iron clad and then steel hulls. The woodland opens out as you near the top of the hill. Oak, beech and conifers give way to bracken and silver birch. At the top of the hill there is a wood of holly on your right and bracken and gorse on your left. Pipers Wait Car Park and Campsite are ahead. Turn left and go to the end of the campsite, over a small gravel bank and onto the heath. Here you are close to the highest point in the New Forest.

Join a gravel path across the heath. For the short route, turn left along another gravel path as you reach the edge of woodland. This will take you back down the hill through lovely old ancient woodland. Otherwise, continue along the track. There are several parallel paths but it doesn't matter which you take as they all tend to converge after a while. You will pass open heath dotted with holly bushes on your left at first. Later there are open bracken and birch slopes to the right as you walk along the ridge top. Where paths meet, look for a path between holly bushes on the left. If you go too far, you will see a broad track at an angle on the left a few metres further on.

This small path widens, crosses an earthbank and then gently descends through ancient oak and beech woods, festooned with mosses, lichens and ferns. Quite a few have suffered storm damage and there is plenty of dead wood around for beetles, fungi and other important wildlife to use. You may even spot holes made by woodpeckers.

The path becomes a little indistinct at the foot of the hill but just keep straight on and you will come to the road near Bramshaw Church. A hundred metres or so to your left you will see the Forestry Commission barrier at the start of the next path. This leads through more woods, past mossy clearings, to a footbridge over the stream. Immediately ahead is a ditch overhung with trees, so skirt this and rejoin the path the other side of the clump. There are a few little paths but your route is straight ahead to the next road. Most of the other paths lead to the road but by a slightly longer route. You should reach Bramshaw Wood Car Park and then follow the road back to the pub.

Walk 3

Pub 1.   **Green Dragon**
Brook,
Near Lyndhurst.
Tel. Southampton
(0703) 813359.

GR 274141   *10-2.30, 6-11.*

P G Play Area. Dogs welcome.
Cottage to let or B & B.
Full Meals 12-2, 7-9.30.

Approximately 600 years old. Two open fires. New Forest pony brands on leather sheets on the walls and ceiling.

Pub 2.   **Bell Inn**
Brook.

Tel. Southampton
(0703) 812214.

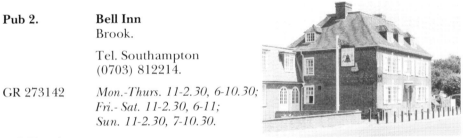

GR 273142   *Mon.-Thurs. 11-2.30, 6-10.30;
Fri.- Sat. 11-2.30, 6-11;
Sun. 11-2.30, 7-10.30.*

P G Play Area
20 bed full accommodation.
Snacks and full meals, 12-2, 6.30-9.30; Sun. 12-2, 7-9.30.
Booking required for parties of ten or more.

The main building, dating back to 1782, has been extended. Its main function now is as an hotel for visitors to the golf courses.

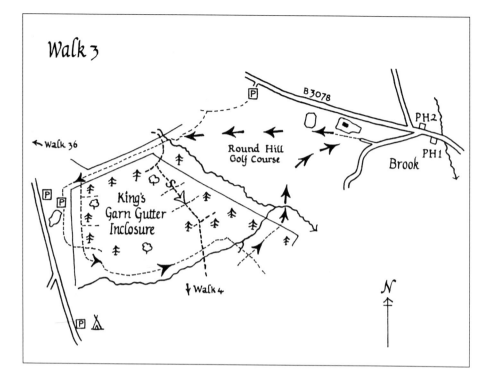

Walk 3　　　**A ROUND OF GOLF**
5 or 6.5 km (3 or 4 miles.)
Links with Walks 4 and 36.

This walk is unlike any other in this book since it includes a complete circuit of a Forest golf course.

From the pubs, go up the hill, passing a sealed Victorian post box in the hedge, and take the lane signposted "Rufus Stone". At the top of the rise, turn right along a gravel track to parking for Roundhill Golf Course. From the end of the car park, keep close to the boundary hedge on the right at first. Then head across the grass, passing the fenced cricket green and keeping fairly close to the woodland on the right. If visibility allows, look on the skyline for a break in the trees - that is the destination of the long route.

You should reach the 14th tee in the corner of the golf course. From there, go down a track and to the right towards a ford across Kings Garn Gutter. Once across, go up and to the left to join a forest road. Ahead is a wide ride between two inclosures. This is your way if you want a long walk.

14

For a short walk, follow the gravel road to the left into Kings Garn Gutter Inclosure. "Garn" or "garden" is thought to be where the royal beehives were placed in the early days. Gutter is the name given to streams in the north of the Forest. Your route then follows tracks and rides through the plantation and brings you to another corner of the golf course.

The longer route steadily climbs the hill. Turn left at the top into the inclosure or carry on a little further to the car park at the top and then go to the left past Janesmoor Pond before entering the plantation. The route back down follows tracks and rides to rejoin the short route.

Leave the inclosure, cross the stream and head across the golf course, keeping close to the wooded edge on the right. Head for Round Hill House on the hill. This will take you back to the members car park and the Rufus Stone road. An open forest location like this results in more than the usual golf course obstacles: New Forest ponies frequently wander around the greens and during the pannage season (October to January) pigs are allowed to roam the adjacent woodland. They eat the acorns and beech mast which are poisonous to ponies if consumed in any quantity.

From the car park, there is a delightful view to the south across farmland to a wooded ridge and the mast at Minstead.

Walk 4.

Sir Walter Tyrrell
Canterton,
Canterton End,
Rufus Stone.
Tel. Southampton
(0703) 813170.

GR 268127   *11-3, 6-11pm winter,*
11am-11pm summer.

P G Play Area. Dogs welcome
Snacks 12-2, 6-10pm, Full meals 12-2, 7-10pm.
Book for restaurant.

Olde worlde atmosphere; hops and farming implements on ceiling; thatched bar; history of the slaying of William the Second, King Rufus.

Walk 4

THE RUFUS STONE AND STONEY CROSS
3 or 6 km (2 or 3.5 miles.) * .
Links with Walks 5, 3 and 36

A short way up the road from the pub, opposite a car park, stands the Rufus Stone. It marks the place and tells how Sir Walter Tyrel shot King William (Rufus) II in a hunting accident in 1100. He is buried at Winchester Cathedral. There is some debate whether William's death was an accident and whether it took place here or somewhere else in the Forest.

The walk climbs a wide grassy slope from the Rufus Stone, passing to the left of a clump of trees and thorn bushes. This slope has a lot of wet patches and especially near a small fenced inclosure, a patch of deceptively deep mud; for a drier route go uphill along the road and then take the track parallel to the dual carriageway which joins up with the route from the Stone. Continue along a wide gravel track, flanked by short turf dotted with gorse bushes.

For a short walk, turn right between holly bushes about 30m before the cottage. The narrow path opens to a more distinct path down the hillside, across grass at first and then through Stricknage Wood. At the foot of the hill, this delightful path follows close to a small stream which winds around meanders between steep banks in the woodland. As you emerge from the woodland, you may see a ford on your left. This is where the long and short routes meet. From here, go diagonally across a wide grassy expanse, skirting a group of trees and crossing a few small streams back to the pub.

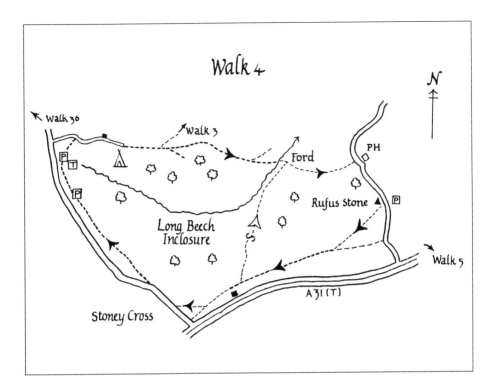

Walk 4

The longer route continues past the cottage beside the dual carriageway, emerging at another road at Stoney Cross. There are lovely views across the Forest from here. Turn right and follow the road to Long Beech Campsite. There are plentiful reminders along here of the wartime occupation – bases of buildings, roads and runways for there was a large airfield here. Most of the troops stationed here were American or Canadian. Much of the New Forest was used either as training grounds or as assembly areas for troops prior to the D-Day invasion of France.

By the public toilets there is a short cut to the campsite. Turn right and walk along the camp site road, past a large green water tower, and continue along a gravel track through beech and oak woods to the ford near the pub.

Walk 5

The Trusty Servant
Minstead,
Near Lyndhurst.
Tel. Southampton
(0703) 812137.

GR 282111   *11-2.30, 6-11;*
Sun. 11-2.30, 7-10.30.

P Dogs welcome. B& B.
Snacks 11-2.30pm

The pub sign is most unusual, copied from a picture in Winchester College. It shows the ideal servant as a pig with a padlocked snout so as not to divulge his masters secrets and hare's feet to enable him to run errands speedily.

Walk 5   POLLARDS AND THATCHES
3 or 5 km (2 or 3 miles.) *.
Links with Walk 4

Minstead is a quiet rambling village with a network of narrow lanes and numerous thatched cottages. You will pass many of these as you make your way to and from the Forest on the long or short circular routes. Because of the indistinct path link to Hungerford Car Park, it is safer to walk these routes anticlockwise.

Close to The Trusty Servant stands Minstead Church. Apart from its own architectural interest, this is also where Sir Arthur Conan Doyle is buried, at the far end of the graveyard. He lived at Bignall Wood nearby.

From the pub in Minstead, walk along quiet narrow lanes, zig-zagging through part of the village and over a small rise to a sharp bend. From here you have one of the best views of Minstead Lodge, an impressive large Victorian house in mock Tudor style. Ahead is Clay Hill and the way for the longer route.

For a shorter walk, turn left towards Suters Cottage. Fork right at the Forestry Commission barrier and follow a path through oakwoods, keeping roughly parallel to the fields on your left. The way can be a little indistinct, so if in doubt bear to the left. You will reach the lane near to Hungerford Car Park.

The longer route, goes straight ahead from the road bend, up and over Clay Hill. You will be passing under ancient beech trees, some of them pollarded - the top of the tree was cut off when it was young to encourage many branches to sprout from one point and therefore produce more timber. This practice was made illegal in 1698 so these pollarded trees must be 300 years old or more.

18

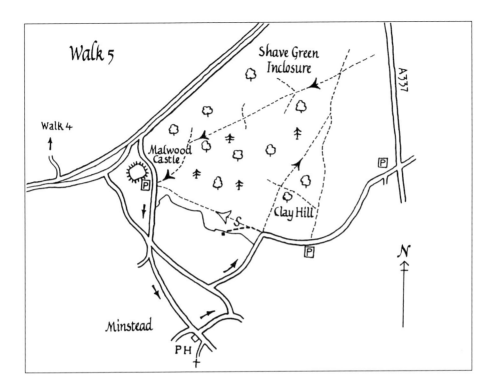

The path descends from the hill top to a grassy clearing. Keep straight on past oak and beech with a glimpse of a grassy lawn on the right at Shave Hat. You will reach a gravel track with gates to right and left. You can see and hear the traffic on the A337. Turn left and follow a straight track that narrows to a path between an avenue of lofty Douglas firs with drooping branches. These large trees were planted in the late 19th century but beneath them are smaller self sown seedlings.

Go through a gate, then the path bends to the left. Keep a marshy, grassy area about 30m to your left. At this point the path becomes indistinct. Keep straight on, going slightly uphill. You should pass some beautifully shaped pollards before reaching the lane near Hungerford Car Park. Up the lane to the right is Malwood Castle, now private flats but reputed to be the site of a royal hunting lodge and the last place King Rufus stayed before he was shot in 1100. To return to the village of Minstead, turn left along the lane and go straight across at the cross roads.

Walk 6

New Forest Inn
Emery Down,
Lyndhurst.
Tel. Southampton
(0703) 282329.

GR 285084   *11-2.30, 6-10.30.*

P G Dogs welcome.
Accommodation.
Snacks and full meals 11.30-2, 6-9.30.

An attractive pub dating back to about 1710 when a caravan was placed on the site having claimed squatters rights. The caravan now forms all of the front lounge porchway and the inn has been extended on either side.

Walk 6   ACRES DOWN
5 km (3 miles.)
Links with Walk 7

Across the road junction, go under an arch and up a narrow road that leads to a number of houses. Follow the road around to the left to the far end. By the last telegraph pole you can see the end of a path at the top of a grassy bank. This leads you through beechwoods, just skirting the summit of James's Hill. You will pass some old gravel diggings on the left as you gently descend. Your path runs between two marshy valleys along a ridge which gently drops down almost to the level of the marsh on the left. Here is a crossing point of paths and an old fence post on the right. To get to the other side of the ridge on the right, fork right a few metres to a track junction then go right by another old fence post. Along here there are many stunted beech saplings - nibbled by deer. After 100m or so, bear left and left again to join a track from the right. Keep left and you will be walking along the edge of woodland with views across a marshy open area (Deadman's Moor) to Acres Down.

Bear right and ford a small stream. Follow the track out of the wood and up the hill to the top of Acres Down. There are fine views all around from here. There are glimpses of Southampton to the east and wave upon wave of wooded hills to the west. To the north are the masts of The Electricity Board at Minstead. To the south is Peterson's Tower in Sway. This folly was built in the 1870's, supposedly to demonstrate the value of concrete as a building material. Other stories suggest it was built as his own memorial and that he received directions for mixing the concrete and laying the foundations from Sir Christopher Wren through a medium. Whatever the truth, it stands out as a major landmark on the south edge of the New Forest.

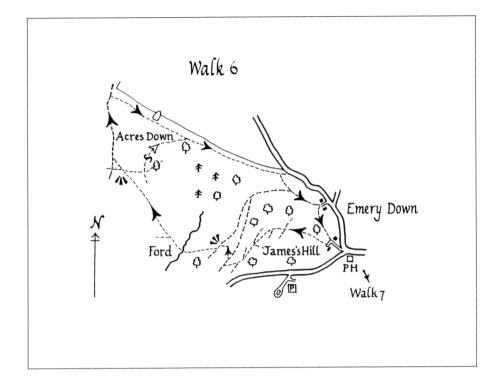

Turn and walk across Acres Down, passing holly bushes neatly trimmed by ponies, and descend to a track following the edge of fields. Below you to the left is a pond decked with lilies in summer. The Forest boundary goes through the middle of it.

Just before reaching the road, turn right across a grassy area to a track through a wood. Follow this leftwards to a small green and an attractive group of houses. Now follow a path through the woods, parallel to the backs of the houses and you will come out on the bend of the small road where you started.

If the first part of this walk seems difficult to follow, you can walk further along the road towards Stoney Cross and start and finish by the little green.

Walk 7

Pub 1.   **Swan Inn**
Swan Green,
Lyndhurst.
Tel. Southampton
(0703) 282203.

GR 291082   *Mon.-Sat. 11am-11pm;*
Sun. 12-3, 7-10.30.

P G Play Area. Dogs welcome.
Snacks and full meals 12-3; Sun. 12-2.30.

Old pub opposite village green and cricket pitch. Real fire.

Pub 2.
New Forest Inn *(see page 20)*
Emery Down.

Pub 3.
Royal Oak *(see page 25)*
Bank.

Walk 7   **ANCIENT FOREST AND THE REPTILIARY**
5 or 6 km (3 or 3.5 miles.)
Links with Walks 6 and 8.

This is a lovely walk through mostly old oak and beech woods. Swan Green makes a picturesque setting for village cricket in the summer. The bend in the main road here is particularly dangerous so do take extra care if crossing this road.

From the gate in the SW corner of Swan Green, a path begins parallel to the main road. After about 100 metres you can fork right and join a wide track. If you miss this small fork, keep parallel to the road and join the track where it reaches the main road. In both cases, turn right up the track and go almost to the top of the slope. You will see a wide path on your left. A few steps take you to the highest point of the path which stretches long and straight before you downhill.

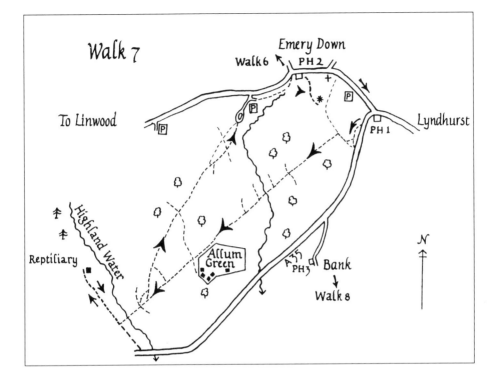

At first you pass ancient oak and beech woods. Beneath these giants is a dense understorey of holly, encouraged for centuries as a year-round source of food for the deer and ponies. In some parts of the Forest there are pure stands of nothing but holly. You can often spot scars or teeth marks on the bark of the trunk or main branches. Sometimes, so much bark is eaten that the holly dies.

As you move further down the slope, the path crosses grassy areas dotted with trees, favourite grazing spots for forest ponies. You pass the cottages and fenced paddocks of Allum Green, a small Forest hamlet, tucked away, out of sight from motorists speeding by on the A35. Where the high boundary wall bends, the main path tends to follow it: take a few steps to the right to see your path. It carries straight on over a small hill and down to a bridge over Highland Water.

A detour of about 1 km will enable you to visit the Reptiliary at the north end of a gravel track. All but one of Britain's native reptiles and amphibians can be found in the New Forest where their heathland and wetland habitats remain intact. The natterjack toad probably existed in small numbers here but has not been recorded since 1950. The harmless smooth snake and sand lizard occur only in small numbers in the Forest. More numerous are the common lizard, grass snake and adder. The Reptiliary consists of a series of walled pits, each containing breeding populations of the native snakes, lizards, frogs, toads and newts. Many of the young are released into the Forest. This is an excellent place to see and learn about these elusive and fascinating animals. A coin-operated listening post and informative leaflets are available at the site. It is open from April to September but is best visited on a hot, sunny day when these cold blooded animals are most active.

Returning from the bridge you will see a fork in the path at the edge of the wood and another a few metres further on. Both meet up at the top of the hill. If you take the first one, keep right after a few paces to go uphill. A lovely path leads you along a ridge, under beech woods and past open areas of bracken, heather and silver birch. After that the path forks. Most of the paths meet up again later but if in doubt, keep to the right each time. You will emerge at James's Hill Car Park.

There is a small path parallel to the road leading to the New Forest Inn and a pavement all the way from there to Swan Green. If you feel adventurous, you could try making your own way, as shown, up the hillside to join a track leading from the pub car park (An alternative starting point) to the Emery Down Reservoir on the top of the hill. From the reservoir tank, go down to another track and turn left. (If you start this walk from The New Forest Inn, turn right along this track.) This track emerges at the road, opposite Silver Street. From here, it is a short walk back to the Swan Inn.

Walk 8

Royal Oak
Bank,
Near Lyndhurst.
Tel. Southampton
(0703) 282350.

GR 286072   *11-2.30, 6-11;*
Sun. 12-2, 7-10.30.

P G Play Area. Dogs welcome.
Snacks available at midday.
Advance notice is advised to avoid possible clash with other bookings.

House records go back to 1719. Log fire in the public bar.

Walk 8

A STEP BACK IN TIME
4 or 6.5 km (2.5 or 4 miles.) * .
Links with Walks 7 and 23

This walk takes you deep into the heart of the forest and beside the headwaters of the Lymington River, almost entirely through ancient deciduous or mixed woodland.

From the back door of the pub, go left along the road to Gritnam, a tiny forest hamlet. You are entering the ancient forest area called Gritnam Wood. It was in these woods that Brusher Mills, the famous snake catcher lived in a turf shelter. (See Walk 24)

As you reach the hamlet, the road forks. For the short route, turn left and take a grassy track opposite a white cottage at the top of the hill. Keep straight on, through a gate to join a gravel track. Just after crossing a stream, turn left along a lovely woodland path. This brings you to a gravel road. Follow this road or a path to the left up the slope to arrive at a small roadside car park. Turn left to return to the pub.

For the long route fork right, cross the stream and take a path through a silver birch copse. This joins another path the other side of a ford. Turn right along that path and go straight on through the woodland, keeping right at the fork. Cross a footbridge and then choose to either turn left and follow the headwaters of the Lymington River or go straight ahead to an area of heathland and Warwickslade Cutting, before returning to the river.

Warwickslade Cutting is an example of the canalisation of streams that took place from 1848-1852 to drain and improve New Forest "lawns" for pasture. Do not go over the bridge but take the path along the edge of the heath. Your route then follows a grassy track past scattered Scots pines, a deer observation platform on

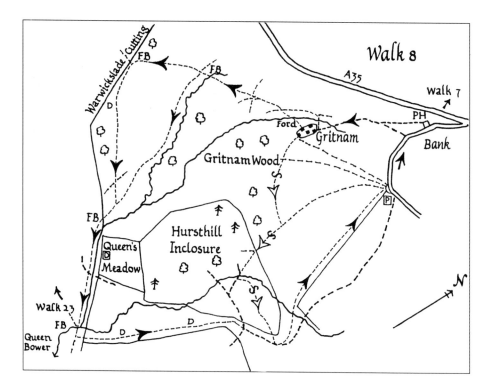

the right and a dense copse of silver birch on the left. Eventually it becomes a woodland track and loses its definition. Keep straight ahead and you will rejoin the track that follows the Lymington River. Go right, cross the footbridge and continue to follow the river.

This will take you past a large, fenced pasture, known as Queens Meadow, and a large deer observation tower. The meadow is a wildlife conservation area. Cross the gravel road ahead and continue to follow the river to the next footbridge. This area is called Queen Bower because it was reputed to be a favourite walk of Queen Eleanor, wife of Edward I, when she visited the New Forest.

Turn left here and take a woodland track that follows an inclosure fence, passing more deer observation platforms. When you reach a gravel road, go straight ahead and rejoin the short route.

Walk 9.

The Crown and Stirrup
Lyndhurst.
Clay Hill,
Lyndhurst.
Tel. Southampton
(0703) 282272.

GR 302069   *11-2.30, 6-11pm,*
subject to change in summer.

P G FR Play Area. Dogs welcome. Real fire.
Snacks and full meals 12-2, 6.30-10pm.
Parties advised to book.

Access to the Forest. The pub takes its name from a stirrup, a replica of which is on display in the Visitor Centre, Lyndhurst. Centuries ago, any Commoner wishing to hunt in the Royal Forest had to have a hound small enough to fit through the stirrup.

Walk 9   THE KING'S DEER
3 or 6 km (2 or 3.5 miles.)

There is direct access from the pub garden onto the Forest. At the back gate, turn right to a gravel road. Turn left then first right along a grassy track. On your right the tall, straight oaks look very different to the solitary oaks in parkland. They are all the same size too - evidence that these were planted.

A grassy ride links Clayhill Car Park with this walk. The woods from now on are a mixture of old oaks and beeches, many damaged by storms with young trees growing up to replace them. Pass a block of pines and go through a gate. A little to the right is a low earthbank. This is part of Park Pale: a wood paling fence once stood on top of this bank, enclosing a two hundred acre royal deer park in 1291. The walks cross or pass other sections of this boundary bank but it is often indistinct.

For the short walk, turn left here and follow the fence to a gravel track. Otherwise, continue ahead, through more ancient and ornamental woodlands and take the second right up a gentle slope. Park Pale embankment crosses the track at the top of the rise. A gravel track now leads on down the slope, past lovely mixed woodland, colourful at any time of the year. This road joins another and then bends to the right. Turn left at this bend and after a few metres turn right down a grassy ride. The ride crosses a small valley then joins another gravelled road. There is an attractive mixture of deciduous and evergreen trees in this part of the wood.

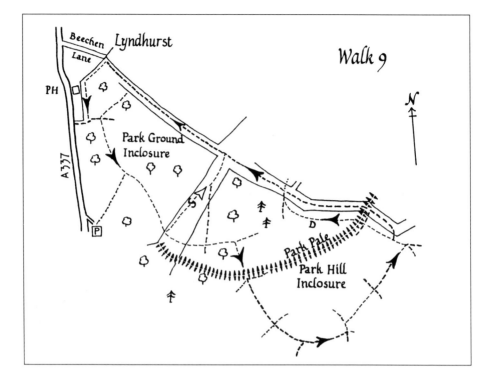

Just before the next junction is a small area recently planted with young native trees. We have thankfully left behind the days when all new planting was of conifers. These young trees have to be well protected from the deer and ponies until they are large enough to withstand their browsing.

Turn left and make a choice - either a grassy ride or the gravel track parallel but out in the open to the right. Halfway along this stretch you cross the Park Pale again. If you chose the ride, you will also pass a deer observation platform. These are used by forest keepers as shooting platforms during the period of deer culling and are not for public use.

The short route joins the gravel track which continues between fenced inclosures. A 2 metre fence like the one on the right is needed to exclude deer. There is a marked contrast between the undergrowth in this inclosure and the open forest, demonstrating the effect that animal grazing has.

Walk 10

Pub 1.   **Waterloo Arms**
Pikes Hill,
Lyndhurst.
Tel. Southampton
(0703) 283333.

GR 298087   *Summer 11.30-2.30, 5.30-11;*
Sat. 11-2.30, 4.30-11;
Sun. 12-3, 7-10.30.

P G FR Play Area. Dogs on leads.
Snacks and full meals 12-2, 7-9.30. Booking advised at weekends.

300 year old thatched pub with collection of antiques and open fire in winter.

Pub 2.   **The Crown Hotel**
High Street,
Lyndhurst.
Tel. Southampton
(0703) 282922.

GR 298083   *Mon.- Sat. 12-2.30, 6-11;*
Sun. 12-2, 7-10.30.

P 40 ensuite bedrooms.
Bar meals/restaurant Mon.-Sat. 12-2, 6-9.30; Sun.12-2, 7-9.
Book for restaurant.

This hotel bears the date 1600 but may go back much further. The present building was designed in 1897 and has real fires.

Pub 3.   **Fox and Hounds**
High Street,
Lyndhurst.
Tel. Southampton
(0703) 282098.

GR 299082   *11-2.30, 6-11.*
Sun. 12-3, 7-10.30.

P (public car park around corner). Patio.
FR Dogs on leads.
Snacks lunch times only. Full meals 12-2 daily and Mon.-Thurs. 6.30-9;
Fri.-Sat. 6.30-9.30; Sun. 7-9pm. Booking strongly recommended Fridays and
Saturdays and most evenings in summer.

Pub 4.   **Stag Hotel**
High Street,
Lyndhurst.
Tel. Southampton
(0703) 283492.

GR 301083   *11-3, 6-11;*
All day in summer.

P G FR for residents. Play Area.
Dogs welcome. B&B.
Snacks and full meals 11-2, 6-11; Teas etc. 2-4 in summer. Booking advisable for restaurant.

Established 1772. A landmark in the High Street. Thought to be haunted.

Pub 5.   **The Mailmans Arms**
71, High Street,
Lyndhurst.
Tel. Southampton
(0703) 282257.

GR 301083   *Mon.-Sat. 11-2.30, 6-11;*
Sun. 11-3, 7-10.30.

G

Snacks 12-2pm. Advance booking required. Barbecues in summer for up to 80 persons.

Large log fire in winter. Collection of crystal and porcelain bells. Special evenings with entertainment and snack suppers.

Nine consecutive years in the Good Beer Guide.

Pub 6.   **Highwayman Bar**
Lyndhurst Park Hotel
High Street.
Tel. Southampton
(0703) 283923.

GR 303082   *10.30-2.30, 6-11.*

P G FR Play Area. Dogs welcome.
59 bedroom hotel.
Snacks 12-2. Booking required for parties of 10 or more.

A very olde worlde bar with low lights and beamed ceiling known locally for the collection of matchboxes on the wall and ceiling.

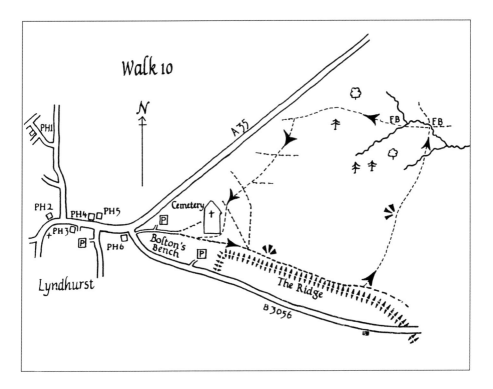

Walk 10   BOLTON'S BENCH AND BEYOND
5 to 6.5 km (3 to 4 miles.) *.

There is plenty of parking space just inside the Forest from the road junction. On a small level area beyond the first car park is a quaint thatched pavilion and cricket green. The small hill crowned with yew trees is called Bolton's Bench after Lord Bolton, Lord Warden of the Forest in 1688. To the left is the cemetery.

A gravel track runs along the ridge top with an old earthbank running parallel to the right. This was probably part of the bank and fence that bounded a 200 acre royal deer park in 1291 (See Walk 9). From this ridge there are fine views across the heaths and woods.

Walk along the ridge, through heather and gorse. Choose any of the parallel paths here. Down to your left, a strip of green stands out amongst the dull browns of the heath - this is Longwater Lawn, a typical forest streamside lawn so popular with the ponies.

The path dips down into a broad hollow. There are some cottages across the road on the right and a wide sandy path leading to the left. Take that path, heading for a clump of pines on a low ridge. If you look left before reaching the pines you will catch sight of the spire of Lyndhurst Church and a large white house (Northerwood House) on the hillside beyond. The church at Lyndhurst is on such a high spot that the spire is often the first thing the traveller sees as he approaches the village.

Go over the ridge and cross a small stream to reach the green ribbon of Longwater Lawn. Ahead is a footbridge and to the right of it an old parish boundary stone. Do not cross the footbridge but follow the stream to the left to cross another footbridge. The path leads across heath into a wood of silver birch, beech and oak. Some of the older trees have been pollarded. As the path approaches the main road the sound of traffic gets more noticeable. When you emerge from the wood and can just see the road, bear to the left, past pines, heather and gorse, heading gently uphill towards a distant clump of large conifers. Soon you will glimpse the church spire. Keep straight on - the clump of conifers border the cemetery and beyond that is the village.

Walk 11

Pub 1.   **New Forest Hotel**
Lyndhurst Road
Ashurst.
Tel. Southampton
(0703) 292319.

GR 334103   *Summer 11am-11pm;*
Winter 11-2.30;
Mon.-Tue. 6-10.30;
Wed.-Fri. 6-11.
Sun. 12-3, 7-10.30.

P G Play Area. Dogs on leads in bar or garden. B&B. Pets Corner.
Snacks and full meals 12-2, 6.30-9.30.
Booking recommended in summer and at weekends.

This was originally built as a hunting lodge and was reputedly used by Queen Victoria and Prince Albert when they visited the New Forest. There is an interesting old fireplace in the bar.

Pub 2.   **The Happy Cheese**
Ashurst Bridge
Ashurst.
Tel. Southampton
(0703) 293232.

GR 336104   *11-3, 6-11.*

P FR (conservatory)
Toby Grill.
Snacks and full meals 12-2, 6-10.
Booking only required in the restaurant.

Lounge has open fires and beamed ceiling with collections of stamps, butterflies and cigarette cards on display.

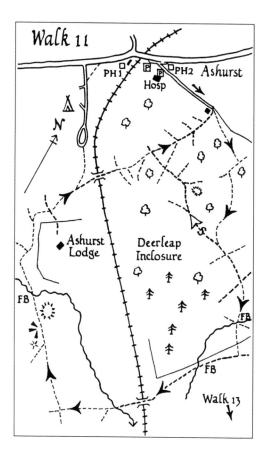

Walk 11   OPEN AND (IN)CLOSED FOREST
3 or 6.5 km (2 or 4 miles.)
Links with Walk 13

The routes are on tracks and sandy paths and can be walked in shoes except after heavy rain.

Start on the east side of the railway bridge, by the Happy Cheese. Follow a gravel road past a cricket green to Churchplace Cottage where the road bends to the right and enters Churchplace Inclosure. Go through the gate and immediately turn left along a forest track past a plantation of oak and beech.

Areas of the New Forest were first inclosed and planted in 1698 when it was realised that there would be a shortage of timber for ships and building if nothing

34

was done. The grazing animals eat the saplings, limiting any natural regeneration of the woodland. The inclosures are fenced to control the extent of grazing.

Both long and short routes pass a hill known as Church Place. The name suggests a former church here, before the creation of the New Forest as a royal hunting area. Other suggestions include the site of a royal hunting lodge. What evidence there is of any structure is well hidden by a cloak of undergrowth beneath old oak and beech trees.

The long route continues through the conifer plantations of Deerleap Inclosure and out onto a broad strip of heather separating it from Longdown Inclosure. Follow a sandy track downhill. Ahead, white railings mark the railway bridge. A raised section of track takes you across Fulliford Bog, then keep right as you go upslope, heading for Matley Wood. For some distance now you cross open heath, passing the lawn of Matley Holms on your left. About 200m before reaching the wood turn right along a sandy track. Where it has worn down into the heath you can see a section through the poor soil that dominates so much of the New Forest. The path passes a few gorse-topped Bronze Age burial mounds, and then on the right a large circular earthwork with a ditch surround.

Beyond the stream rhododendrons mark the boundary of Ashurst Lodge on the right. Keep close to the fence and around the corner you come to the road leading to the lodge. Cross where there are low Car Free Area barriers and follow a track straight ahead through natural oak and beech woods to a railway bridge.

Either go over the bridge and follow a grassy ride and tracks back to Churchplace Cottage or do not cross the bridge but take the path to the left and follow the railway line back to the campsite and then a path across the grass to the New Forest Hotel.

Walk 12

Beaulieu Road Pub
Beaulieu Road Hotel
Beaulieu Road
Lyndhurst.
Tel. Southampton
(0703) 293344/45/46/47.

GR 350063   *11am-11pm.*

P G FR Play Area. Dogs welcome. Hotel accommodation.
Special area with hitching posts for horses.
Snacks and full meals during opening hours.
Booking for parties of 15 or more required.

Walk 12   A RAILWAY THROUGH THE HEART
5 or 8 km (3 or 5 miles.) * .

A small railway station on the Southampton to Bournemouth line, in the middle of the Forest? It seems an odd place but the answer lies in part across the road. Wooden pens stand empty for most of the time but, for a few days each year, this place is packed with people and ponies for the New Forest Pony Sales. The route of the railway was largely dictated by the Forest Inclosures at the time (1847). (See Walk 21)

To begin the walk you must first cross the railway line to Shatterford Car Park. Set off from there along a well defined sandy track parallel to the railway. Across the expanse of heath to the right are a few Bronze Age burial mounds. The route crosses a marshy valley bottom and then passes a railway bridge on the left. Soon after that on a slight rise you may spot a long, heatherclad earthbank about 1 to 2m high. This is known as the Bishops Dyke. According to legend, a representative of the Bishop of Winchester was promised as much of the New Forest as he could crawl round in 24 hours. The dyke is said to represent his route and until quite recently the marshy land within it was owned by the Bishop of Winchester.

At a fork in the path, at the edge of the woods, turn right for a short walk or left for an extra 3km (2 mile) loop. Now follow the boundary fence of Denny Lodge Inclosure. Cross over the railway bridge and turn right through a gate. For the next kilometre or so your way is along grassy tracks and paths through Frame Heath Inclosure to a level crossing at Woodfidley Cottages. It is in this part of the New Forest that you are very likely to see Sika deer. These animals are slightly larger and greyer than the more common Fallow deer. Walk quietly and look along the rides for them.

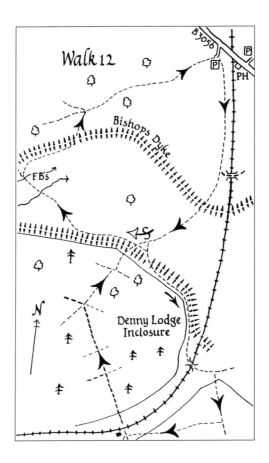

Cross the railway and go straight ahead up and over the ridge, through Denny Lodge. On the far side of the ridge, head NE along grassy rides to a gate and join the short route within sight of the deciding fork. Two deep, circular holes either side of the ride are probably craters caused by stray bombs during the last war.

Follow the path westwards, keeping parallel to the inclosure fence at first. The path swings away from the fence line and ahead are a series of footbridges. Scan the woods to your left for signs of fallow deer before you reach Denny Wood ahead. A few metres beyond the last footbridge, turn right and make your way along a fairly indistinct path, keeping close to the edge of the wood. Storm damage may mean a few detours around fallen giants. The path climbs a short slope and joins a wider path leading from Denny Lodge, back to the pines of Shatterford Car Park.

Walk 13

The Bold Forester
Beaulieu Road
Marchwood.
Tel. Southampton
(0703) 865967.

GR 377085   *11-3, 6-11.*

P G FR Play Area. Dogs welcome.
Skittle alley.
Snacks and full meals 12-2, 7-10.
Booking required for restaurant.

Walk 13

CONIFERS AND CONTRABAND
4 or 8 km (2.5 or 5 miles.)
Links with Walk 11.

From the pub your route is along a quiet country lane bounded by wide verges, old hedges and deep ditches, leading to Foxhill Farm. From the farm, take a grass path to the left, keeping the inclosure boundary about twenty metres to your right. Go over a small rise to an area of grass and mature pines, reminiscent of parkland. Go through the gate on the right and take the left fork.

A beautiful grassy ride leads you around the hill between the pines of Ipley Inclosure. You can make a short detour as far as a gate for a view across the moorland or go through the gate and cross the grass to the banks of the Beaulieu River and the boundary of Ipley Manor. The track continues up a gentle slope. At the gate turn right to return to the pub.

From this high point you can see the lane leading back past the pub towards Marchwood. This is possibly a route used by smugglers between Cracknore Hard and houses such as Ipley Manor. Sometimes the horses would be shod back to front to mislead customs officers. As late as 1873 a smuggler was caught with contraband off Cracknore Hard.

For a longer walk, go straight ahead to the edge of the pine trees. A gravel path leads you across open heath towards Longdown Inclosure. Most of the route in this inclosure follows gravel tracks. At one junction I have indicated a choice of routes either continuing along gravel tracks around the hill or via a track of soft forest earth and pine needles over the hill.

Shortly after leaving the inclosure, a raised path crosses a boggy area. Here you can safely see the colourful array of flowers and mosses that thrive in these conditions - the soft, pink flowered cross-leaved heath, yellow spikes of bog

38

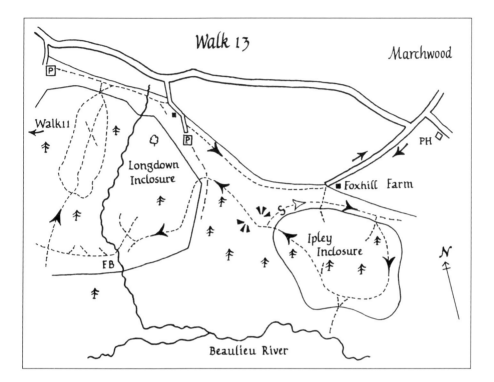

Walk 13

Marchwood

Walk 11

P

P

Longdown
Inclosure

FB

Foxhill Farm

PH

Ipley
Inclosure

N

Beaulieu River

asphodel and perhaps the tiny red-tinged rosettes of the insectivorous sundew. Inside a small fenced area, purple moor grass, bog myrtle and heather have grown tall - an indication of what the heathland would look like if it were not grazed.

When the path peters out, bear left up the hili. This brings you to a lane leading past a converted chapel to Longdown Car Park. Follow the lane, the boundary of the New Forest, back to Foxhill Farm.

Walk 14

Pub 1.   **The Heath**
Beaulieu Road
Dibden Purlieu
Hythe.
Tel. Southampton
(0703) 842275.

GR 412059   *Mon.-Sat. 11am-11pm;*
Sun. 12-3, 7-10.30.

P G FR Play Area. Only Guide Dogs welcome.
Snacks available all day in summer. Full meals 12-2, 6.30-10pm.

Pub 2.   **Gleneagles**
Butts Ash Lane
Hythe.
Tel. Southampton
(0703) 842162.

GR 419058   *11-3.30, 5.30-11.*

P G Play Area.
Snacks and full meals at lunchtime.
Booking required for Sunday lunches.
Real fire. Golf memorabilia.

Walk 14   DIBDEN INCLOSURE - BATS AND BILBERRIES
3/4 or 6/7 km (2/3 or 3.5/4.5 miles.)
Links with Walk 16

The Forest is diagonally across a roundabout from The Heath. Alternatively, start from the Forestry Commission Car Park. On the north side of the car park is a shallow rectangular hollow, a relic of past gravel extraction. Take the track that runs along the north edge of this. When you reach a low point with ditches and often a large puddle, turn right and follow a path that undulates and curves along the edge of the pine plantation. To your left is an open marshy valley. It is quite possible to find yourself being observed by a deer from the pine and oakwoods on the other side of the valley. The path joins a wide track. There are lovely views from the gate before you descend to cross the marsh of Dibden Bottom.

For a short walk, turn left when you reach the woods and go up the slope between mature oakwoods (The Noads). Later in the summer there is a carpet of bilberry that rarely reaches more than a few inches high because of the grazing by ponies.

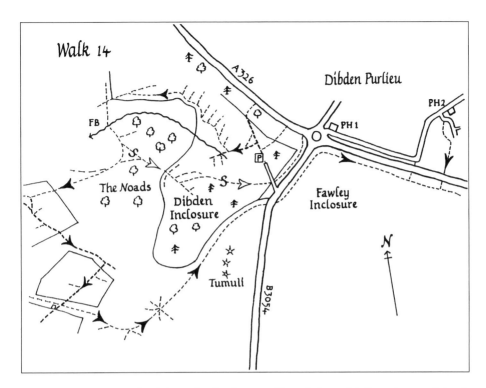

The route takes you back into the Inclosure. Turn left and follow the track back to the turning to the car park from the road.

The long route turns right after crossing Dibden Bottom and heads for Kings Hat Inclosure, forking left halfway across the heath. Go into the plantation, round a sharp bend and follow the forest road across wet heath. In summer, look for patches of red on the ditch sides - closer inspection will reveal groups of sundew, an insectivorous plant that obtains its food from insects caught on its sticky leaves.

The road bends sharp right past pine trees, some of which have clusters of bat boxes high upon their trunks. These provide roosting sites where there is a shortage of suitable hollow trees. On your right, at the next track crossing, there is one the many pony pens in the Forest. The ponies are driven into these for marking or to select some for pony sales.

Now you climb back up the hill side onto the plateau that dominates the landscape between Waterside and the Beaulieu River and return across the heath, noting a pair of gorse covered tumuli (Bronze Age burial mounds) on the right.

Walk 15

Pub 1. **The Old Mill Inn**
Limekiln Lane
Holbury
Southampton.
Tel. Southampton
(0703) 891137.

GR 427041 *Winter 11-3,6-11;*
Summer all day.

P G FR Play Area. Dogs welcome.
Snacks and full meals 12-2, 7-10.

14th century thatched mill cottage and 17th century barn. Log fire. Haunted by the ghost of a monk.

Pub 2. **Bridge Tavern**
Ipers Bridge
Rollestone Road
Fawley
Tel. Southampton
(0703) 892554.

GR 425031 *11-2.30, 6-11.*
Variations in summer.

P G Play Area. Dogs welcome.
Snacks and Full meals 12-2, 7-9.

Real fire.

Walk 15 ANCIENT TRIBES AND DARK WATER
4, 3 (*) and 6 (*) km. (2.5, 2 and 3.5 miles)
Links with Walk 16

There are several short walks in this area that could also be combined into longer ones if wanted.

A. From The Old Mill Inn a new, well signposted footpath leads along the stream valley, following an old boundary bank for some distance before reaching a lovely lake ringed with trees and reeds. Continue on, over numerous stiles, around the hillside and diagonally across the grass to the field corner at the boundary of the

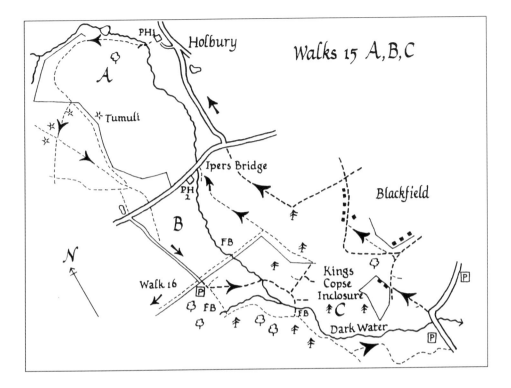

New Forest. Close by and ahead are a number of tumuli - Bronze age burial mounds, often standing out on the heathland because of their cover of gorse. They are particularly numerous in this area. Most have been disturbed in the past and are hollow in the centre but, unlike rich burial sites elsewhere in the country, these contained little more than charcoal and the occasional clay urn.

Follow the path to the Beaulieu - Blackfield Road. From here you can either return along the lanes, or cross the road and continue across the heath into Kings Copse Inclosure for Walks B and C.

B. The stream that flows through the middle of this Inclosure is called Dark Water because of the dark reddish brown stain in the water, derived from the soil. The inclosure is planted with conifers making a pleasantly shaded walk on a hot summers day or a place of shelter from the cold winds of winter. Along the wider paths sunlight bathes the grassy verges, encouraging a wealth of wild flowers and butterflies in summer. Cross the stream and return up the other side of the valley, emerging through mature oak and beechwoods onto open heath again. Follow the gravel path up a small hill, passing old shallow gravel workings on the left. From the top of the hill there is a lovely view north across the Bridge Tavern to a large house and riding stables and the flat topped heathland beyond.

This heathland, dotted with gorse bushes, is the habitat preferred by the rare Dartford Warbler, Britain's only resident warbler. The heathlands of Hampshire and Dorset are the last refuges of this tiny bird. Their numbers fluctuate with the winter weather, hard winters taking a heavy toll of their small population. Look out for a small grey and brown bird perched on top of a gorse bush or tall heather, flicking a long tail up and down and singing noisily.

When the gravel path peters out, make your way downslope through the bracken and silver birch trees to the stream. You will have to step across it to reach the gate by the road.

C. If you choose to walk the longer route, continue along the wooded valley then climb a short steep hill and follow the path to the road and car park. The road crosses Blackwell Common, a lovely area of heathland and the haunt of many dragonflies and damselflies in summer. Turn left up a track and follow a green lane. These old routeways are real gems in our modern countryside. Often bordered by ancient hedgerows, they act as corridors for wildlife and have an air of timelessness about them. The last part of the route follows a quiet country lane back to the Blackfield Road. Cross this to reach the Old Mill Inn or turn left for the Bridge Tavern.

Walk 16

The Royal Oak
Hilltop,
Beaulieu.
Tel. Beaulieu
(0590) 612228.

GR 401032   *Easter - Sept. All day or
11-3, 6-11.*

P G Play Area.
Snacks and full meals 12-2, 6.30-9.15.

Between Beaulieu Museum and Exbury Gardens. There is a large forest lawn in front of the pub which attracts forest ponies, donkeys and cattle.

Walk 16   A FOREST LAWN AND OPEN HEATH
4 or 6.5 km. (2.5 or 4 miles.)
Links with Walks 14 and 15

From this pub the flat plateau of heathland stretches out before you. Gorse, heather and a few stunted trees dominate the landscape and yet there is much more of interest for those who look.

After about two hundred yards you will see a large rectangular expanse of grass, seemingly out of keeping with the natural heath vegetation. This is one of the forest "lawns" and dates back only to the 1940's. During that period there was a shortage of food and much marginal land was ploughed up, including about 1000 acres of the New Forest. The soils are naturally poor so fertiliser was added and crops such as potatoes and barley were grown. The land was reseeded and returned to open grazing. Today, such expanses of short turf are popular picnic sites as well as favourite grazing for the ponies.

Gravel paths lead you across the heath with several route choices indicated on the sketch map. For a short walk, make your way to the Blackfield Road and then return along its verge. For a longer walk, cross that road and pick up a well defined track running across the plateau. The stacks and towers of Fawley Power Station and Refinery are a distinct feature of the skyline. In the opposite direction it is possible to pick out the relatively small Bronze Age burial mounds that abound in this area.

At first sight you appear to be walking through a sea of heather and gorse but look again: the short cropped turf holds a wealth of tiny wild flowers of white,

45

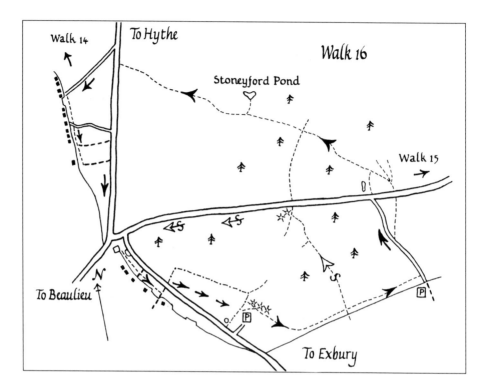

yellow and blue – gems in a sea of green. Gorse has a reputation for being able to flower any time of the year but its main season is May. Then the air is heavy with a scent, some say of coconut, others of bananas. You can make up your own mind. By late July or August the seed pods are ripe and explode open in the summer sunshine, scattering the seeds. The crackling sound is reminiscent of a bowl of cereal.

Take care crossing the road to Hythe and then follow a track beside a line of houses representing forest edge encroachments in the past, before returning to the road.

Walk 17

Pub 1. **Turfcutters Arms**
Main Road, East Boldre,
Beaulieu.
Tel. Beaulieu (0590) 612331.

GR 374004   *Mon.-Fri. 10.30-2.30, 6-11;*
Sat. 10.30am-11pm;
Sun. 12-3, 7-10.30.

P G Play Area. Dogs welcome.
Full meals and snacks 12-2, 6-10. Booking advised.

The pub name refers to one of the Commoners' rights - that of cutting peat for the fire. On one wall in the pub are peat cutting spades. The original building was a thatched cottage with a path linking it to the coast. Smugglers hid their contraband in the oven.

Pub 2. **The Wine Press**
Montagu Arms Hotel,
Beaulieu.
Tel. Beaulieu (0590) 612324.

GR 388023   *Mon.- Sat. 10.30-2.30, 6-11;*
Sun. 12-3, 7-10.30.
All day Sat. and Sun. in summer.

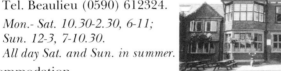

P Full hotel accommodation.
Full meals 12-2.15, 6.30-9.30.

The pub is part of a large, attractive hotel in the heart of the village. There was an inn here as early as the 13th century when the abbey was founded.

Walk 17   OF FLYING MACHINES AND MONKS
6 to 6.5 km. (3.5 to 4 miles.)

If you start at the Turf Cutters, you will soon pass a village hall which was once a YMCA canteen for serving men during the First World War. Behind it lies an open area of heath and close to the hall can be found traces of buildings and a road - all that is left of the first airfield in the New Forest.

In May 1910 the New Forest Flying School was set up by a wealthy American from Philadelphia, J.Armstrong Drexel, and a local man "Motor Mac" McArdle, who had a garage in Bournemouth. Two sheds were erected on the east side of the road, one for the Bleriot and one a workshop. On fine evenings the plane would be pushed across the road to "take the air". After setbacks in France during World War One, the government took over the airfield for flying training. There were frequent accidents and many deaths while training, witnessed by gravestones in East Boldre churchyard. The airfield finally closed after Armistice in 1918.

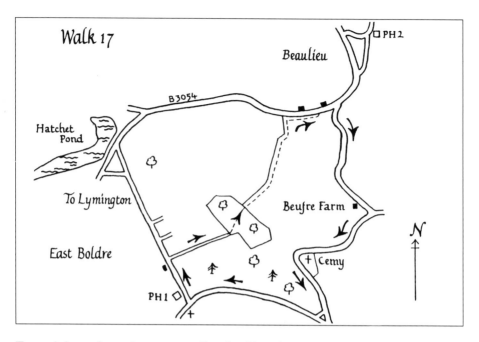

Turn right and continue past a Baptist Church to the end of Chapel Lane. A path leads through a delightful little wood of oak and coppiced hazel. Coppicing - cutting trees off near ground level to encourage multiple shoots - was a traditional form of woodland management that is only now being recognised for its value to wildlife. After 15 years of growth, the poles would be cut and used for fencing, charcoal, etc. From the wood, the route follows a public right of way along the edge of fields and then follows a short stretch of the Beaulieu-Lymington road before turning to follow quiet country lanes back to East Boldre.

You may like to make a short detour into the picturesque village of Beaulieu. Across the tidal mill pond are the remains of Beaulieu Abbey, founded in 1204 by King John as a Cistercian monastery. Most of it was destroyed during the 16th century Reformation.

Continuing our route, you next pass Beufre Farm which occupies the site of one of the granges that, from the 13th century, supplied the monks of Beaulieu Abbey with grain (oats and wheat). The name Beufre suggests that it was also a centre for plough oxen. Today there is an impressive barn of brick and timber, possibly dating back to the 18th century. A quiet lane leads past fields and small copses to Grindingstone Cottage on a sharp bend, opposite Beaulieu Cemetery. The road crosses a stream and cuts up through a wood to a junction. Turn right here along Cripplegate Lane back to East Boldre church and the pub is on your right.

Walk 18

East End Arms
Lymington Road
East End
Lymington.
Tel. Lymington (0590) 65223.

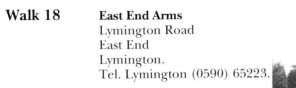

GR 362968   *11-3, 6-11.*

P G FR Play Area. Dogs welcome.
Snacks and full meals during opening hours.
Please book in advance if possible.

An old cottage style pub with a real fire and a haunted bedroom.

Walk 18   THE SOLENT WAY
2 or 5 km. (1.5 or 3 miles.)

This corner of the Forest has a pleasant blend of old and new, giving it a traditional feel.

A one hour walk takes you along a country lane flanked by old hedges and banks of flowers in summer, then follows a part of the Solent Way, a 60 mile walkers route from Milford on Sea to Emsworth, near Havant. This walk crosses fields and mixed woodland. From the fields there are panoramic views across the Solent to the hills of the Isle of Wight. In winter, the fields between here and the shore are popular roosting sites for flocks of waders at high tide.

The walk can be extended further along the Solent Way with a detour to Sowley Pond. Sowley Pond has been of local importance for centuries. In Medieval times, the monks at Beaulieu valued it as a source of fish. In the 17th and 18th centuries its water provided power for an iron works, first a blast furnace and later a forge as well. Around 1750, Sowley was supplying guns to the East India Company. Today it is a tranquil place, home or resting place to many varieties of duck. With binoculars, you can also pick out the tree top nests of herons on the north side of the pond. these fascinating birds can sometimes be seen patiently waiting at the waters edge for a fish or frog to pass by.

Return along the same path to the main route which continues along a straight track through more woodland, the grassy rides decked in wild flowers from spring to autumn. The north section of this wood is of hazel coppice. Coppicing is a woodland management tradition that has sadly gone into decline although an increasing number of landowners are realising the benefits of this system for wildlife and timber production. For the first few years after each cutting the coppiced woodland floor is a carpet of flowers in spring.

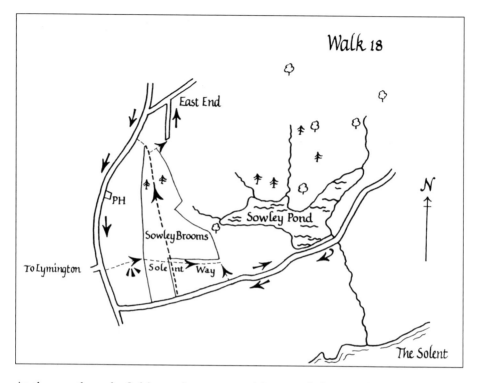

At the north end of this track you may either cut left over the fields towards Bridge Farm and return to the pub , or extend the walk a little by turning right. This takes you into Rowes Lane where you will see an assortment of cottages, some still of the traditional cob construction (clay and straw). The lane brings you out to the heath by the Norleywood Road junction. Opposite the phone box stand two houses named The Old Bakehouse and Old Post Office - testimony to village life in the past when local shops and services were more widespread. Follow the lane around to the left and it will take you back to the pub.

Walk 19

Fleur-de-Lys Inn
Pilley,
Near Lymington.
Tel. Lymington
(0590) 672158.

GR 328982   *11-2.30, 6-10.30.*

P G FR Dogs welcome.

Snacks and full meals. Last orders 2pm for lunch, 9.30 in the evenings, 1pm and 9pm Sundays. Booking required.

This was originally a pair of Foresters cottages, the tree roots and fireplace opening (an old New Forest Rights tradition) can still be seen in the stone flagged entrance passage. The French connection goes back to the time of William the Conqueror who rewarded his supporters with tracts of land. Pilley was later passed on to William de Vernum. A former window in Boldre Church once bore his Arms which included a Fleur-de-Lys. The two bars are named after characters from the book "The Children of the New Forest" by Captain Marryat, first published in 1847.

Walk 19   BOLDRE CHURCH AND THE FOREST EDGE
3 or 5 km. (2 or 3 miles.) * .

From the main street, turn up Chapel Lane. Once you are past the houses, this becomes a quiet country lane, bounded by thick, ancient hedges and banks of flowers in summer. You can try estimating the age of a hedge very simply by counting the number of different woody species (oak, hazel, elder, etc) that occur in 30 m lengths of the hedge. A rough rule of thumb is one species for every hundred years. Of course, some hedges were planted with a mixture of species. However, some of these hedges may have been in place for 500 years or more.

At the fork you may wish to detour a little to visit Boldre Church, dating from the 12th century. Inside is a portrait of William Gilpin, vicar from 1771 to 1804 and author of the book "Remarks on Forest Scenery", first published in 1791. He did much for the village, including setting up schools for 20 boys and 20 girls and endowed them with the proceeds of the sale of his drawings and sketches.

Also in the church is a painting and book of remembrance for the crew of HMS Hood. This was the flagship of Vice Admiral L.E.Holland who went down with it in action against the Bismarck in 1941. He regularly worshipped at the church so his wife arranged for the memorial to be set up here. An annual service is held here on the nearest Sunday to 24th May, the date of the sinking.

From the fork the short route turns right along a footpath to a wood. For the longer route another path links the church with the gravel track towards Dilton Farm. At the next junction, bear right towards Little Dilton Farm and then left past a cottage where the track sides have been planted with hundreds of daffodil bulbs.

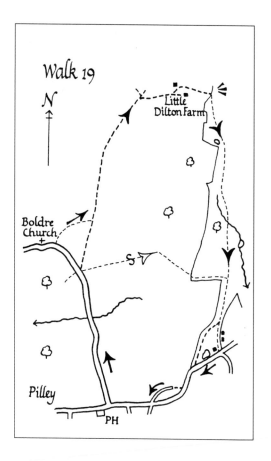

Walk 19

N

Little Dilton Farm

Boldre Church

Pilley

PH

When you emerge onto the open expanse of Beaulieu Heath, you have a clear view across a flat plateau of heather with the woods of Hawkhill Inclosure to the N and Norley Inclosure to the SE. It is so flat here that it is no wonder that it was chosen as the site of an airfield during World War II.

Now the path roughly follows the Forest boundary. You skirt a shallow pond and then cross under a line of telegraph poles. You will pass a small, deep pond on the left of the path, possibly a bomb crater. Continue down a funnel shape of grass between fields. Keep to the left as it narrows and you will pass a lovely pair of thatched cottages. Turn right at the road to the village pond. Its origin is suggested by the name of the adjacent cottage: Gravel Pit Cottage. A final detour across grass to join the end of May Lane will take you past some delightful thatched cottages normally hidden from view.

Walk 20

Pub 1. **The Filly Inn**
Lymington Road,
Setley,
Near Brockenhurst.
Tel. Lymington (0590) 23449.

GR 303003   *11-2.30, 6-11.*

P G FR Dogs welcome outdoors.
Snacks and full meals 12-2, 7-10.
Booking not necessary.

Traditional New Forest inn, full of old beams, brass and country implements. Reputed to be haunted by an old highwayman.

Pub 2. **The Hobler**
Southampton Road,
Battramsley,
Lymington
Tel. Lymington (0590) 23291.

GR 307991   *11-2.30, 6-11*

P G FR (in summer garden shed).
Play Area. Dogs in garden.
Snacks and full meals 11-2, 6-10. Booking advised in evenings.

Real fire. Wine Pub of the Year 1986,'87,'88. BFFA Caterer of the Year 1989. Guinness Caterer '89 Runner Up. Assortment of animals in the garden.

Walk 20   BAT BOXES AND MODEL BOATS
5 or 8 km. (3 or 5 miles.)
Links with Walk 21

Many pubs can be reached by old footpaths and these are no exception. East from the Hobler, the route uses rights of way beside woods, across fields and between houses until it enters Brockenhurst Woods. This is an extensive area of mostly mixed deciduous woodland that, in contrast to the New Forest, has not been grazed by ponies and cattle for a long time. As a result there are many plants on the forest floor that are generally absent from New Forest woodland. This Site of Special Scientific Interest is owned and managed by the Hants and Isle of Wight Naturalists' Trust.

From the hill top at Sandy Down, a lovely woodland path winds down the other side of the hill. To one side is a boundary bank and ditch clothed with mosses

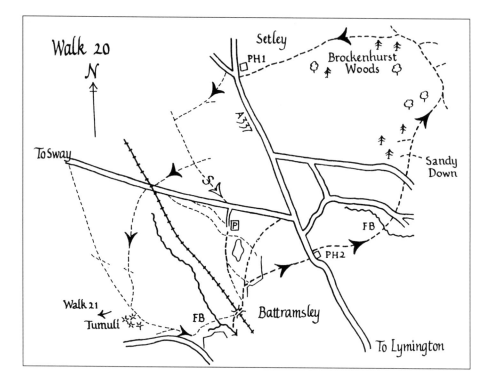

and ferns. This joins a track which you then follow for the next mile. As you round the bend of this track, a public path leads off to Brockenhurst past some magnificent old oaks.

Once you are on the long, straight stretch, heading for the A337 and Filly Inn, look out on your right for groups of bat boxes fixed high on the trunks of pine trees. These boxes are intended to encourage bats to roost here. Although they are similar in size and shape to bird nest boxes, the opening is in the bottom so that these amazing animals can climb up into the box. Each tiny Pipistrelle bat eats over 3,000 small insects a night, so they are very welcome.

Cross the main road and follow gravel paths across New Forest heathland down to a railway bridge, then climb the slope to the ridge top. (If you walk this route in reverse it is easy to miss this path to the railway bridge and you may join the road further along as shown on the map.) About one third of the New Forest consists of heathland. Much of it is artificially maintained by regular cutting or controlled burning. This removes old, tough plants and encourages tender fresh growth which forms an important part of the diet of New Forest ponies. Such management also destroys tree seedlings which, if allowed to grow, would gradually take over the heathland and create woodland in its place.

On the ridge top the sandy path passes several gorse covered Bronze Age burial mounds. The route takes you downslope again and back over the railway to a lake, a flooded gravel pit, set aside for model yacht sailing.

From here, there are fine views across the heaths with Peterson's Tower on the skyline to the SW. This 220ft tower was built on the south side of Sway in the 1870's by Andrew Peterson, a former Judge of the High Court of Calcutta. It has twelve rooms, one above the other, reached by a spiral staircase at the side and is one of the first buildings ever to be constructed of concrete. Why it was built remains something of a mystery. It has remained empty for many years but plans are now afoot to turn this local landmark into a hotel.

From the corner of the rough grassy area, a narrow footpath between hedges leads straight back to the Hobler.

For a shorter route from the Hobler or Filly Inn, bear left on the way across the heath to the railway line and rejoin the route at the lake.

Walk 21 Hare and Hounds
Durnstown,
Sway.
Tel. Lymington
(0590) 682404.

GR 283987   *11-2.30, 6-11.*

P G FR Play Area. Dogs on leads.
Full meals 12-2 weekdays throughout the year;
7-9pm Fri.and Sat. and all week in summer.

Real fire. Collections of old photos of Sway area, Guinness pictures and banknotes from around the world.

Walk 21 RAILWAYS ACROSS THE FOREST
5 km. (3 miles.) *
Links with Walk 20

West from Brockenhurst, three railway lines spread out across the forest, one of them now dismantled. The first railway line across the Forest was the Southampton to Dorchester Line, opened in 1847. It was built mostly due to the enthusiasm of a Wimborne solicitor A.L.Castleman but had to twist and turn on its way to Ringwood and Wimborne in order to reduce damage to the existing inclosures. This gave rise to the name "Castleman's Corkscrew". West of Brockenhurst, this line was closed in 1963 following the Beeching Report. The main line to the west is now the more direct Bournemouth line opened in 1888 to serve that fast growing town. A third line was built south to Lymington in 1858 and remains in use.

From the pub, head north and turn right at the war memorial. Go past a playing field and turn left along a grassy gap. At the field corner take the wide path slightly to the left, heading for the road. After crossing a wet area, the path veers to the right and goes along the side of the hill. Across the heath to your right runs the Lymington Branch Line.

Cross the road, then the main Southampton to Bournemouth railway line to another road. Ahead is a broad track running up the side of a wooded hill. To the right across the heath is Cater's Cottage. A path starts in a group of pussy willow trees just across the road and winds its way between the heather and gorse to emerge on a track a little to the right of the cottage.

From the cottage either follow the dismantled railway line through the cutting or continue around the back of the hill for the views to the north. If you choose the latter then follow the track past the cottages and around the hill towards Hinchelsea Wood. About halfway across the heath there is a path junction by a

56

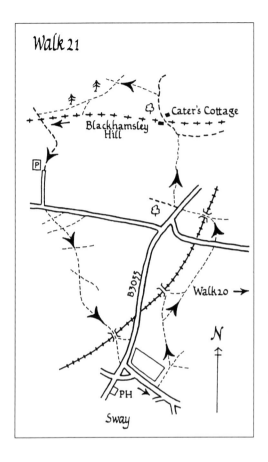

small group of trees. Go left here towards the line of telegraph poles. Bear left under the telegraph line to get onto the disused railway line or continue parallel to them to a junction by a dismantled bridge.

From here, go straight up a broad gravel track to Longslade View Car Park. Stop here for a moment to take in the view to the right. A wide grassy "lawn" spreads out down to the old line and beyond is the grassy valley of Long Slade Bottom, backed by a skyline of inclosure plantations.

Cross the road and head slightly to the left along a path that widens as it goes downhill towards the village of Sway. When you are very close to the houses on the right and low down in the valley, the path turns uphill to the left to a bridge over the railway. Ahead and a little to your right is the war memorial and the pub where you started.

Walk 22

Forest Bar
Forest Park Hotel,
Rhinefield Road,
Brockenhurst.
Tel. Lymington
(0590) 22844.

GR 293027   *11-2.30*

P G Children and dogs welcome.
38 en suite bedrooms.
Snacks 12-2, full meals 12.30-2.
Booking required for full meals.

Real fire, own grounds to rear and riding stables adjacent to hotel.

Walk 22   RHINEFIELD AND OBERWATER
3 or 6.5 km. (2 or 4 miles.) * .
Links with Walks 23 and 24

Start the walk from Beechern Wood Car Park, 750m west of the Forest Park Hotel or about 1.5 km. (1 mile) from the village centre.

Take the gravel road that skirts the fields and leads to the Aldridgehill Campsite. Alternatively, go as far as the bend and then take the path down to the Oberwater and follow that river to the campsite.

For a short walk turn left here to the cottage then left again to follow a route through Aldridgehill Inclosure and back to the car park. Otherwise, go through the campsite, then look to the left for a path heading across the grass towards the woods. You should see a round pond. Keep it on your right and the path will lead you to a footbridge. From this grassy area you get your first views of Rhinefield House over the tree tops to the west. More footbridges follow, the path leading through a wet wood aptly named Fletchers Thorns. You cross the straightened channel of Fletchers Water and take the left path past an area of hummocky grass. Go diagonally across grass to a gate. A grassy track soon leads to a gravel track. Go left if you wish to shorten the walk a little and avoid roadside walking. Otherwise follow the route to the right, along tracks to the Rhinefield Ornamental Drive.

A roadside walk takes you to Rhinefield House. There has probably been a dwelling on this site since the New Forest was created in 1069. A succession of forest keepers lodges occupied the site and by 1859 it was the home of the nurseryman who planted the conifers of the Ornamental Drive and Rhinefield

58

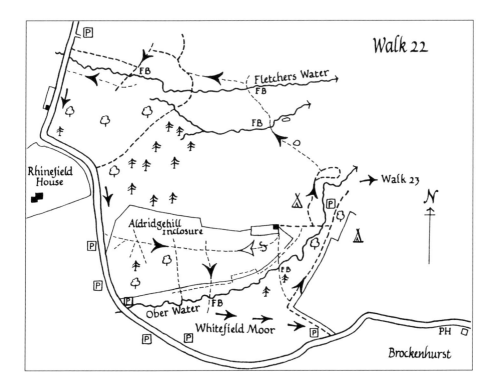

Grounds. In 1877 many of the Crown Lands were "privatised" and Rhinefield became the property of the Walker family. In 1885 their only daughter became engaged to Lt. Munro and was given £250,000 to build a new family home at Rhinefield after the marriage in 1887.

The great House was lavishly furnished and decorated by skilled craftsmen, reflecting the personal tastes that the Walker-Munros acquired in their travels. It included four suites for the daughters that were planned. Unfortunately they only had one son. He inherited the house but when he died in 1950 it had to be sold. Since then it has had a chequered history as a school, a hotel and apartments and conference centre.

The walk continues along tracks through Aldridgehill Inclosure then turns right down a path to a footbridge over Ober Water. The coloured posts and wayside information plaques are part of a Forestry Commission Trail, Ober Water Walks, that begins at Whitefield Moor Car Park. Keep left across the grassy expanse of Whitefield Moor to return to Beechern Wood Car Park.

Walk 23

Pub 1.   **Rose and Crown Hotel**
Lyndhurst Road,
Brockenhurst.
Tel. Lymington (0590) 22316.

GR 303024   *Summer 11am-11pm;*
Winter 11-2.30, 6-11.

P G FR Dogs welcome on lead in pub
or garden, B&B. Snacks and full meals 12-2, 6-10.
Barbecues in summer. Booking advised for evenings and Sunday lunches in the
restaurant.

Pub 2.   **Foresters Arms**
10, Brookley Road,
Brockenhurst.
Tel. Lymington (0590) 23397.

GR 302022   *11-2.30, 6-11;*
Sun. 12-3, 7-10.30.

P G Play Area. Dogs welcome.
Snacks and full meals 12-2 throughout the year,
evenings only in summer.

The building used to be a blacksmiths workshop.

Pub 3.   **The Snakecatcher** *(see page 63)*
Lyndhurst Road.

Pub 4.   **The Morant Arms** *(see page 63)*
Brookley Road.

Pub 5.   **Forest Bar** *(see page 58)*
Forest Park Hotel.

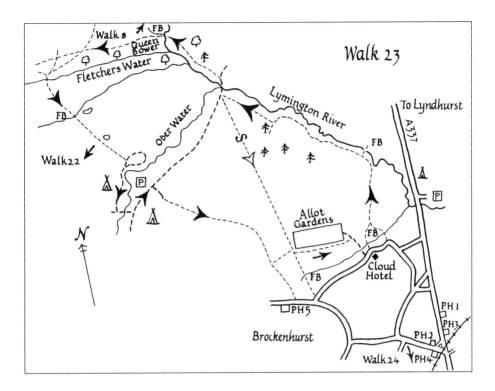

Walk 23   THE LYMINGTON RIVER

3 or 6.5 km. (2 or 4 miles.) * .
Links with Walks 8, 22 and 24.

Start on the road bend by the Cloud Hotel. Use a footbridge to cross the stream and then head across the grass towards the woodland that borders the river. You should spot a track leading straight into the woods and cross another footbridge. Keep straight on, picking your way around fallen trees until you come to the river – only a matter of 50 metres. There is a wooden footbridge across the river. Do not cross this but turn left and follow this beautiful stretch of the Lymington River along its bank - this may involve some scrambling over or around fallen trees.

The river flows in broad, sweeping meanders with deep pools and shallow riffles. The gravel and sand bed is visible through the yellow-brown water, stained that colour from the soils of the district. Eventually you reach a cross track. Turn left and immediately right to follow a straight path beside an old boundary bank and ditch, just inside the edge of the wood. This will take you to a track junction where Bolderford Bridge is visible to the right.

For a short walk, turn left here and use a straight, raised path across the open heath of Black Knowl that leads to the allotments. As the path passes beside the allotments, there is a marked ridge and furrow pattern on the grass to your right. It would be nice to think that we have discovered a medieval field system, but it is the result of ploughing and drainage during the last war. Many areas of the New Forest were dug up and cultivated for grain or potatoes at that time. At the top of the rise, turn left and follow a bank to the allotment road and back to your starting point.

The longer route crosses Bolderford Bridge and follows the river as far as a lovely wooded area known as Queen Bower, so named because it was a favourite walk of Queen Eleanor, wife of Edward I. Cross another footbridge and turn left across Poundhill Heath towards Poundhill Inclosure. After a short distance beside the inclosure fence, bear left. The path narrows between a woodland dominated by thorn bushes, aptly named Fletchers Thorns.

The first footbridge crosses Fletchers Water, a tributary of the Lymington River, straightened to improve drainage. Continue over several more footbridges to a broad expanse of heath. Keep straight on, heading for the Aldridgehill Campsite. Beyond the campsite road is woodland flanking the Ober Water, another tributary of the Lymington River. You can either ford this and go straight to Ober Corner Walkers Car Park or detour to the right along gravel roads. From Ober Corner, continue down a road towards a private campsite and then along a path to the allotments where you join the short route.

Walk 24

Pub 1.   **The Snakecatcher**
Lyndhurst Road,
Brockenhurst.
Tel. Lymington (0590) 22348.

GR 303023   *Mon.-Fri. 11-2.30, 6-11;*
Sat. 11-3, 7-11; Sun. 12-3, 7-10.30.

P G FR Play Area Dogs welcome Skittle Alley
(bookings only).
Snacks and full meals 12-2, 7-9.30.

*Collection of jugs and collection of prints about Brusher Mills, a local hermit who collected
snakes from the Forest to sell to zoos.*

Pub 2.   **The Morant Arms**
33, Brookley Road,
Brockenhurst.
Tel. Lymington (0590) 23333.

GR 303022   *11-2.30, 6-11.*

P G Play Area Dogs under strict control B & B.
Snacks and full meals 12-2, 7-9.

*Pub is right beside level crossing and during the summer
the "Orient Express" stops at Brockenhurst once a week. Named after the last family that held
Brockenhurst Manor.*

Pub 3.   **Foresters Arms** *(see page 60)*
Brookley Road.

Pub 4.   **Rose and Crown Inn** *(see page 60)*
Lyndhurst Road.

Pub 5.   **Forest Bar** *(see page 58)*
Forest Park Hotel.

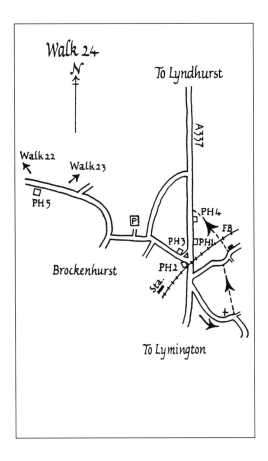

Walk 24   BRUSHER MILLS AND BROCKENHURST CHURCH
1.5 km. (1 mile.)
Links with Walks 22 and 23

From the centre of Brockenhurst this makes a pleasant half hour circular stroll.

Head for the station and cross the level crossing. This is the main line from London to Bournemouth, built in 1847. Commuters from here may enjoy a unique view of the New Forest as the train twists around "Castleman's Corkscrew" between the inclosures and across the heaths towards Southampton (see Walk 21). Ignore Mill Lane on your left but take the next lane left gently uphill to the church. There are features of interest in both the church and the graveyard.

This is the oldest church in the New Forest. Beside the church stands an enormous yew tree, thought to be about 1000 years old. The oldest part of the present building is the carved arch of the south porch which dates from the twelfth century and is an excellent example of Norman craftsmanship. Inside, the font is also Norman. In the lower part of the south wall the stonework is arranged in a herringbone pattern, typical of Saxon building, suggesting an earlier church on this site.

In the north east corner of the churchyard you can find the carved headstone to "Brusher Mills", a local character who lived in the forest in a shelter made from branches and turf. He got the name "Brusher " because he used to brush the Forest cricket squares. He died in 1905 but for 21 years he made a living clearing out snake nests. Some snakes were sold to London Zoo and some to local chemists since adder fat was used for all manner of remedies. A life size model in the New Forest Museum, Lyndhurst depicts his life style.

Just beyond the churchyard there is an entrance to the grounds of Brockenhurst Park, part of the land belonging to Brockenhurst Manor which once stood here. We turn left down a track between high hedges to Mill Lane. On your right is an impressive arched gateway to the Park. Go diagonally across the lane to follow another track that leads to a footbridge over the railway and down a short lane to the Rose and Crown Inn.

Most of the village of Brockenhurst lies on the east side of the main road. If you have time, it is worth strolling around the rambling lanes. You will discover a delightful blend of old and new. In parts, houses and cottages spread around little greens, footbridges or fords across the streams that flow through the village and thick hedges and cattle grids protect many front gardens from the attention of the ponies and donkeys that roam through the village.

Walk 25

The Rising Sun Inn
Bashley Common Road,
Wootton,
New Milton.
Tel. Ringwood (0425) 610360.

GR 243984   *Mon.-Sat. 11-2.30, 6-11;*
             Sun. 12-3, 7-10.30.

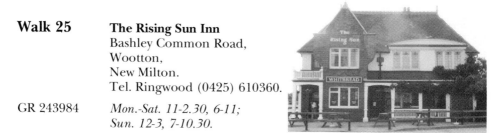

P G FR Play Area. Dogs welcome except in restaurant.
Snacks and full meals 12-2; Weekends 12-2.30, 7-9.

Listed in the "Doomsday Book". Thought to have been a staging post.

Walk 25   PONIES AND POTATOES
5 or 6.5 km. (3 or 4 miles.) * .

From the pub, go along the road towards Tiptoe as far as the bend. Here a track branches left along the edge of a large furrowed grassy expanse. You can either follow this for about 350m then turn left by a copse towards Broadley Inclosure, or take a short cut across the grass straight to the Inclosure. If you choose the short cut, be prepared to wind your way through a maze of pony paths between the gorse bushes that form a wide band between the grass and the Inclosure.

The furrowed pattern is the result of ploughing and drainage during the 1939-45 war: about 1000 acres of the New Forest were permitted to be used for cereal or potatoes at that time. Those cultivated areas were then reseeded and have been maintained as "lawns" by the dunging and grazing of ponies and cattle.

A short route skirts the southern edge of the plantations, rejoining the longer route at Wootton. Broadley Inclosure is a pleasant mixture of deciduous and coniferous trees. The main track tends to be popular with riders so at times it may be easier going through the trees just off the track in places. The route brings you out to Wootton Bridge Car Park and picnic site beside the Avon Water. Its gravel bed and tendency to a rapid rise in water level after heavy rain is typical of New Forest rivers.

From here, either take the gravel track through Wootton Coppice Inclosure or from the river bank follow a grassy path outside but parallel to the Inclosure fence. The path route can be very muddy in places in winter. If you walk the path in spring you will in places be surrounded by snow white blackthorn blossom. Eventually the path meets a track near a ford. Turn left, past more thorn bushes and small oaks stunted by persistent grazing, to meet the gravel track.

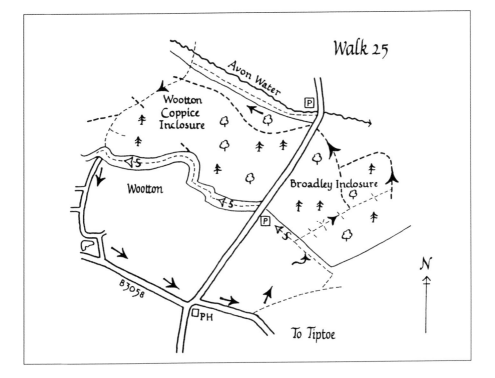

Walk 25

Go gently uphill along tracks to a field boundary. A little to the right, cross a ditch and follow a dirt road past the cottages and paddocks of Wootton, turning sharp left at a large pond. The road bends to the right and then you emerge onto grassy heath with the pub visible in the distance to the left. Cross the grass, aiming for the pub and you will pass a large stone trough. Here we have a mystery for the inscription on the side tells us that this was presented to the Corporation of Brighton in 1887 as a memorial. There is no clue as to why it should have ended up in the New Forest.

Walk 26

Pub 1.   **White Buck Inn**
Bennets Lane,
Burley.
Tel. Burley (04253) 2264.

GR 224027
P G FR Dogs welcome. Hotel accommodation.
Snacks 12-2, 7-9. Full meals available in summer.

Pub 2.   **The Queen's Head** *(see page 70)*
The Cross,
Burley.

Walk 26   OLD AND NEW TIMBER INCLOSURES
5 or 7 km. (3 or 4.5 miles.)
Links with Walk 27

From the inn, turn left along Bennets Lane then turn right along Southfield Lane, past an assortment of cottages. Go right along Bisterne Close, passing a holly wood. Holly has always been very important as food for the deer and other herbivores. Its evergreen nature makes it particularly welcome in winter and many stems bear the scars of pony teeth. It was actively encouraged throughout the New Forest and dominates the woodland in some places.

Turn left down a gravel track, past two cottages and then passing in front of a pretty thatched cottage. Keep close to the field boundary to join another track. This track leading through Shoot Wood has been turned into a gully by heavy rain so follow it as best you can to the edge of the wood. A broad path then crosses the heath to Rooks Bridge where a footbridge helps you across Mill Lawn Brook. Go on up Redrise Hill through more holly to an open heathy area on the top. As the path starts to go downhill there is a junction. Look along it to the left and you will see a gate in the Inclosure fence. This is the way for the short route, following the fence outside the Inclosure.

Go straight on for the longer route, crossing a small stream, to a gate. To your left, in a corner is a deer observation platform. From the gate, go slightly left and follow a ditch or the edge of a larch plantation uphill. To your right and on top

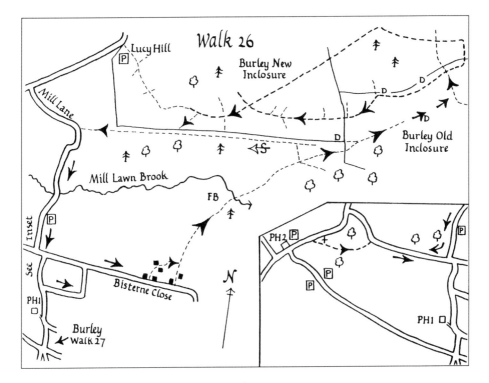

of the hill is the ancient oak and beech wood of Burley Old Inclosure. There are some fallen trees on the summit so keep to the left near the larches and go gently down to a grassy track. Go left down this to a gravel forest road.

Turn left along this road for about a mile to a forest cross roads. You are now in Burley New Inclosure with more conifer plantations. In sunny spots on the side of the road you will see the incredible mounds of pine needles that are each home to millions of wood ants. In winter the anthills tend to collapse and many are probed by green woodpeckers for tasty morsels but in spring the ants begin rebuilding, gathering materials and food from tens of metres away.

Turn left at the cross roads then fork left at the second junction along a track to the woodland edge. Here you rejoin the short route and continue along the inclosure edge and across the grass to Mill Lane. Go left along Mill Lane, over a ford or footbridge and past a car park to the pub.

Walking this route from the Queens Head in the centre of the village will add on about 2 km or 1.5 miles. An inset on the map shows the shortest route via the church.

Walk 27   **Queen's Head**
The Cross,
Burley.
Tel. Burley (04253) 3423.

GR 212031   *Mon.- Sat. 11am-11pm;*
Sun. 12-3, 7-10.30.

P FR Dogs by outside seating.
Snacks and full meals 12-2, 7-9.30pm.
Booking required for large parties.

This pub dates back to the 17th century and was known to be a meeting place for smugglers. Indeed, a smugglers horse is reputed to be buried beneath the flagstones near the bar and there are reported sightings of the ghost of a local smuggler, possibly Peter Warne coming to check his horse. It was not altogether surprising then, when alterations a few years ago revealed a secret room for storing contraband.

Walk 27   **SMUGGLERS TALES**
3 or 5 km. (2 or 3 miles.)
Links with Walk 26

With woodland reaching down to the shore, the New Forest provided ideal conditions for smugglers to land their goods. There are many tales of smugglers paths and hiding places across the forest. Tubs of brandy were often sunk offshore, to be floated ashore later. Heavier barrels were often run up the rivers and sunk in forest ponds. They were raked out on moonlit nights so the smugglers became known as the "Hampshire Moonrakers". Your walk begins at a smugglers haunt and passes along sunken lanes, perhaps used by smugglers in days gone by.

This walk explores the ridge to the west of the village. To reach it you must first walk about half a mile along Pound Lane past a few shops and tea rooms. Just past a post box and opposite an old green lane, turn right up Castle Hill Lane. The track leads up a gentle gradient onto the ridge. Oak and beechwoods fall away to your left. From the top there are views towards Ringwood across rolling moors and waves of wooded ridges and valleys.

Further on there is a broad platform of mature oak and beech trees. This is Coffins Holms. Beyond that are fields on the left and Black Bush Cottages on the right. Just before the cottages is a stile. This is the short route back to the village.

Otherwise continue along the ridge top to Castle Hill. This is a flat grassy area, bounded by high banks and ditches. It was a fortified settlement about 2,000 years ago, with clear views for miles across the heaths. From the far banks you can look out over Vales Moor and the road to Knaves Ash and Crow from Burley

70

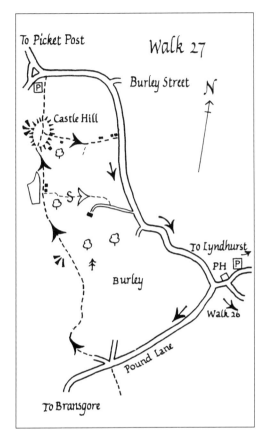

Walk 27

To Picket Post

Burley Street N

Castle Hill

S

To Lyndhurst

PH P

Burley

Walk 26

Pound Lane

To Bransgore

Street. Beyond is the ridge with Smugglers Way running along the top of it. To the north is a mast on Verely Hill which figures largely in another smuggling tale.

Lovey Warne and her brothers, Peter and John, lived in a cottage at Knaves Ash and acted as guardians of Smugglers Way. Lovey used to smuggle lace and silks by wrapping them around herself under her clothes. She also helped by walking the Verely Hill ridge in a scarlet cloak to warn other smugglers of Revenue men nearby.

To return to the village, go back to the main path and continue along it a few yards to a road. Follow the road to the right and then along a track down hill. In places the track is deeply cut between high banks. It emerges on a surfaced road serving Castletop Bungalow. There you join the road back into the village along a safe footpath for the road at times is also cut deeply into the hillside.

Walk 28

Red Shoot Inn
Tom's Lane,
Linwood,
Ringwood.
Tel. Ringwood (0425) 475792.

GR 187094 *Mon.-Sat. 11-2.30, 6-11;*
Sun. 12-3, 7-10.30.

P G FR Play Area. Dogs welcome. Adjacent to camp site.
Snacks and full meals 12-2, 7-9. Bookings advised.

Real fires and old beams. This was originally the village post office and garage! The pub name is linked with the culling of Red Deer.

Walk 28

RED, ROE AND FALLOW DEER
4 or 7 km. (2.5 or 4.5 miles.) * .
Links with Walk 29

Opposite the pub is an area of grass. Go to the far left corner to find a track and then a path off to the left through oakwood and holly. This will take you safely to Amies Corner.

Turn right along a forest road, past Roe Cottage and into Roe Inclosure, a patchwork of conifer plantations and mixed woodland. The road crosses a stream and goes upslope. On the right is a large, circular embankment called Castle Piece. The short route goes through the middle of this and down to a stream then turns along the valley, fords Linford Brook and returns upslope and over the ridge through old oakwoods.

The long route continues along the road to a junction within sight of a gate ahead. Turn sharp right and immediately left down a track that follows a boundary bank and ditch on the right. At the inclosure boundary you suddenly have a wide view of open heath of heather and grass and a skyline dominated by the A31(T).

Go over the footbridges and up the long slope towards the road. Near the top the heath changes suddenly - a reminder of the devastating fire in the summer of 1989 which burned deep into the soil. It will take many years for this scar to heal.

Turn right at the top. The landscape stretches away for miles towards Fording-bridge. Go downhill to Pinnick Wood and fork left. In winter, when the bracken is down, you can see a small circular embankment on the left - possibly the

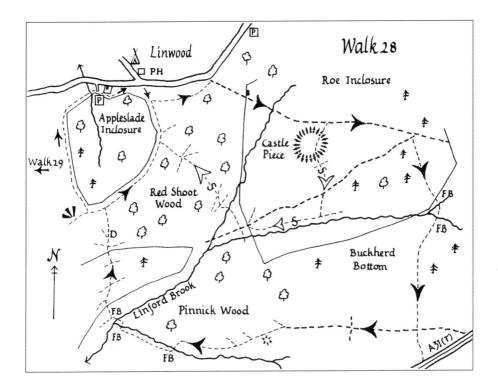

remains of an 11th century enclosure for pigs at night during the pannage season. Keep forking left, staying near to the edge of this old oakwood and close to the stream.

After passing a ford, turn left over a footbridge and follow the stream across a forest lawn. Cross a small footbridge and walk along a short path to a larger bridge over Linford Brook. Ahead is Great Linford Inclosure. The blue topped posts are part of a School Trail. Continue through the Inclosure and soon you will be among the old oaks of Red Shoot Wood where, despite its name, you are more likely to see fallow deer. Take the path uphill past a deer observation platform to a track along the ridge top.

Choose here how to return to the pub. Go right along the track through woodland or go left, with a brief detour to the hill top for the views, and then take a grassy path around the outside of the wood to Appleslade Walkers Car Park. Follow the fence from the car park and behind the cottage you will discover one of the pony pens that are dotted across the Forest.

Walk 29

Alice Lisle Inn
Rockford Green,
Near Ringwood.
Tel. Ringwood (0425) 474700.

GR 159081   *Summer 11am-11pm;*
Winter 11-2.30, 5-11.

P G FR Large Adventure Playground.
Pets Corner. Dogs welcome.
Snacks and full meals 12-3, 6-9.30; Afternoon teas, etc. 3-6 in summer.

Booking for the restaurant recommended in summer. Until 30 years ago this was a schoolhouse.
It has many original beams and a large log fire. The pub takes its name from a local lady who
became famous because she was sentenced to be burned to death, for treason, by Judge Jefferies
at Winchester. Her crime was harbouring two supporters of the Duke of Monmouth, on the run
after his defeat at the Battle of Sedgemoor. She appealed to James II for clemency but he just
changed the method of death. She was beheaded on September 2nd 1685 and is buried in
Ellingham churchyard.

Walk 29   MOYLES COURT AND IBSLEY COMMON
5 or 6.5 km. (3 or 4 miles.) * .
Links with Walks 28 and 30

The pub now stands on an apron of land, flanked on three sides by flooded gravel
pits. Nearby, older flooded workings are used by a growing number of water
sports enthusiasts. The area of the New Forest near here is privately owned: these
walks are therefore designed to use only public rights of way.

Begin by following the lanes to Moyles Court School, formerly the home of Dame
Alicia Lisle after whom the pub is named. The boundary of the grounds on the
left hand side of the lane is marked by a ditch with one side walled. This is called
a ha-ha and acted as a barrier to livestock without interrupting the view.

Just past the school, fingerposts point the way through a gate and up across the
fields. The next kilometre or so of the route runs along the foot of an undulating
hillside that marks the edge of the plateau of Ibsley Common. From these
bracken and heather covered slopes there are fine views west across expanses of
water and the Avon valley to Ringwood Forest.

The path joins a rough track by a house at Mockbeggar. Go down to the left,
across two streams to a dirt road. Cross this and go straight up a short steep bank
to join a path and follow this left around Summerlug Hill, behind a few cottages.
The path becomes a track and after turning right at the next junction, you come
to a large flat area - a former gravel pit. Ahead is a clump of pines - Whitefield
Plantation. Follow the embankment to a track up the slope at the far end.

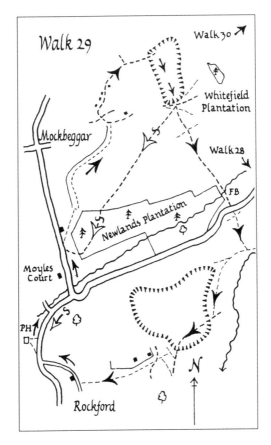

Go straight over the first track to a path junction after about 50m. For a short walk, head towards the right hand end of Newlands Plantation on the skyline. From there you will go down a steep slope and across a field to the gate by Moyles Court. The long walk goes straight ahead, giving wonderful views that change all the time. The path goes steeply down to cross Dockens Water. Cross a road and climb the valley side onto Rockford Common.

After another 150m, turn right at a junction and follow a track beside Whitemoor Bottom, a small marshy valley. Keep left and you will find yourself on top of an embankment with another large abandoned gravel pit on your right, now covered with gorse and grass. The path dips to cross part of the hollow. At the top of the next slope, turn right and then left. Your route now follows the boundary of a group of houses and will take you down a wooded slope to fields. Go straight down towards a thatched cottage and walk along the lane to a cross roads. The pub is on your right.

Walk 30

Royal Oak
Old Ringwood Road,
North Gorley,
Fordingbridge.
Tel. Ringwood (0425) 652244.

GR 161119   *Mon.-Fri. 11-2.30, 6-11;*
Sat. 11-3, 6-11;
Sun. 11-2.30, 7-10.30.

P G FR Play Area. Dogs on leads.
Snacks and full meals 12-2 (Sat. 2.30), 7-9.30.

17th century thatched pub with oak beams and real fire, opposite village pond.

Walk 30

OVER THE HILLS AND FAR AWAY
5 or 7 km. (3 or 4.5 miles.)
Links with Walks 29 and 32.

Much of this edge of the New Forest is enclosed and farmed. To reach the wide open heathland you must cross two small ridges.

Opposite the pub a green lane provides a summer route up onto the first hill but is very wet and more a stream bed in winter. An alternative is to go up the lane towards Hungerford. Where the green lane meets this road, there is limited parking on old gravel workings. This is effectively your starting point.

From the parking area, take the left hand path which leads up onto a bank. These hill top gravel workings, like many others along this edge of the New Forest, are now abandoned and overgrown with gorse and grass. They make a fine home for numerous rabbits. About 50m before you reach a house and road, turn sharp right and follow this path down a green lane between pastures to a footbridge over Latchmore Brook. Cross a lane and go straight up the other side of the valley, past a farm, onto Dorridge Hill. There is a small wood on your right but you continue up through bracken onto an expanse of heather. Ahead of you stretch mile upon mile of rolling moor and woodland.

Go straight ahead but, for a short route, turn sharp right at the first junction. This will take you back to the wood where you will find a road leading gently downslope to the lane below Furze Hill.

Continue ahead for the longer route, down into a hollow and then a little to the right, gently downhill. Just before you reach a stream, swing right between gorse and bracken, up and over a small rise, keeping almost parallel to a line of

76

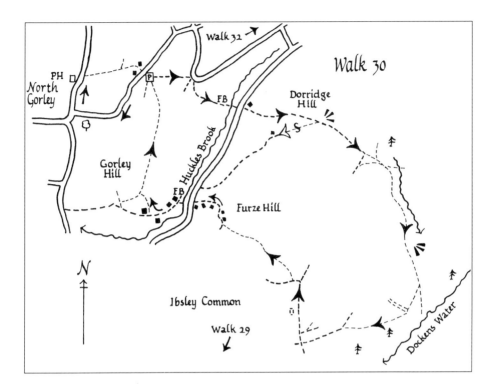

Walk 30

telegraph poles. Now the path takes you along the foot of an undulating slope towards Dockens Water. Bear right and right again through the heather until you cross a double track leading straight up the hillside. Cross this and follow the path which climbs the slope at an angle. At the top, keep left along the edge of the plateau, heading for a large clump of pines (Whitefield Plantation). After 200m turn right along a major track, heading for the end of a line of telegraph poles and passing two small ruins.

At the next cross track, take the second left which will take you past a small gravel pit before descending to a group of cottages below Furze Hill, one of them a thatched cob. Across the next road a footbridge takes you to a dirt road. Follow this to the left and after the bend, take a steep path up to the right onto Gorley Hill. Turn right at a path junction and then go straight across the large abandoned gravel pit to the rough parking area where you started.

Walk 31

High Corner Inn
Linwood,
Near Ringwood.
Tel. Ringwood (0425) 473973.

GR 196108

Mon.-Fri. 11-2.30, 6-11;
Sat. All day; Sun. 12-3, 7-10.30.

P G FR Play Area. Dogs welcome.
Woodland chalet, B&B.
Snacks and full meals 12-2.30, 7-10.

Real log fires in winter. Collection of bank notes on beams in top bar, match boxes on beams in lower bar.

Walk 31

A FOREST PATCHWORK
4 or 7 km. (2.5 or 4.5 miles.) * .
Links with Walks 32 and 36

The landscape of the New Forest is often described as a patchwork of heath, grass and forest. This walk, especially the longer route, takes you through a lovely mixture of these "patches".

Start just below the pub and follow the edge of the wood across the grassy area of Nices Hill to a footbridge over a small stream in Amberslade Bottom. Go left into Broomy Inclosure, an area of plantations - mostly conifers but also some beech. Follow the forest road uphill and along to a gate. On the other side of the gate there is a dramatic change to old oak plantation with a bracken covered forest floor and much more light and space under the trees. For the short route, turn left at the next junction and return beside the stream or along the track.

Continuing on to a cross roads, turn left, down towards Dockens Water and then past Holly Hatch Cottage (See Walk 36). Beside the stream is a typical ribbon of lush grass, so popular with the forest ponies. Cross the footbridge and follow the gravel track up Ragged Boys Hill to woodland edged with holly. Here is a fine view point along the valley.

Go into the wood and fork left and left again. This will take you past many yew trees with dark red fluted trunks. Another ridge top path approaches yours from the right and goes parallel for about 200m before joining. Soon the path crosses a ditch which bounds a square platform, named on maps as The Churchyard but thought to be the site of a Royal hunting lodge in the thirteenth to fifteenth centuries. It would have had a magnificent view from this ridge-top position.

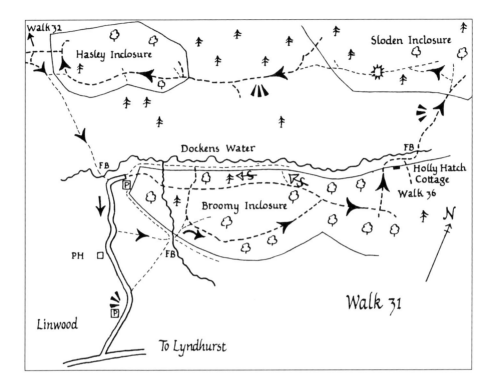

After another 200m keep left and pass to the left of an impressive pollarded oak with numerous, huge branches issuing from one point. Go left down the slope and ahead is the gravel track crossing the heath towards the woods of Hasley Hill. There are excellent views across rolling heath: ahead is Ibsley Common and to the right Hampton Ridge and Frogham.

Your route takes you into Hasley Inclosure, a mixture of oakwood and conifers but there is something different as the track bends. On the right is a fenced area of coppiced Sweet chestnut. For centuries this practice has produced plentiful poles for fencing and fuel.

Turn left at the junction to leave the inclosure and join a sandy track that leads down to the footbridge at Woodford Bottom. It is a short walk from here back up to the pub.

Walk 32

Foresters Arms
Abbotswell Road,
Frogham,
Fordingbridge.
Tel. Fordingbridge
(0425) 652294.

GR 173129   *11-3, 6-11; Sun. 12-3, 7-10.30;*
All day Sat. in summer.

P G FR Play Area Dogs on leads.
Snacks and full meals 12-2, 7-10 Mon - Sat; 12-2, 7-9.30 Sun.
Parties advised to book.

One of the oldest pubs in the New Forest.

Walk 32   HAMPTON RIDGE AND LATCHMORE BROOK
4 or 6.5 km. (2.5 or 4 miles.) * .
Links with Walks 30 and 31.

From the pub, walk due east to Abbots Well where there is a car park and scenic views across the area you will be walking. Continue downhill to a sharp bend where you take the wide gravel track heading left uphill. On your right is a small rise called Windmill Hill. An alternative, short route would be along the middle path a little to the right of Windmill Hill summit, but this can be marshy in places and entails fording Latchmore Brook.

You gradually climb past gullies and old small gravel pits to the top of Hampton Ridge. There is a white concrete pillar on the left - a trig. point used by surveyors to construct accurate maps. As usual, this is situated where there is a particularly wide view of the countryside. To the right, in the valley bottom, a large grassy area stands out against the heather slopes. Your path will be crossing it later.

The expanses of heather in the New Forest are maintained by grazing and controlled burning. This reduces the growth of tree seedlings and gorse yet encourages fresh heather shoots which are more palatable to the ponies. It is in some senses an unnatural landscape - if left alone, the heathland would in time be replaced by birch and pine and eventually oak woodland.

Continue along the ridge to a junction where you fork right. The wide path leads across the ridge and then down into the shade of Alderhill Inclosure. Go straight down the tracks, cross a ford and leave the inclosure through a small gate. Turn right to follow Latchmore Brook all the way down to Ogdens Car Park.

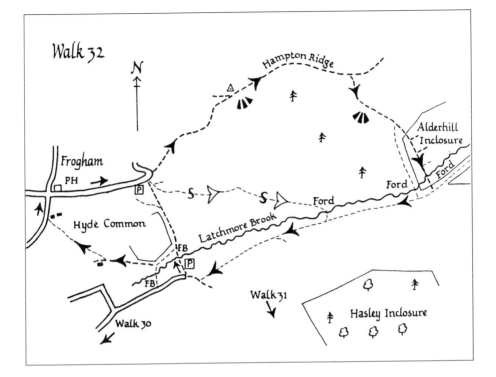

The large grassy "lawn" that your path crosses is one of many that have been fertilised and reseeded in an effort to improve the grazing of the Forest. Rabbits abound here and in winter you may also see flocks of migrant birds such as fieldfare and redwing.

From Ogdens Car Park, you can either go straight uphill to Abbots Well Car Park or cross the footbridge and immediately turn left alongside a fence, pass a ford and continue up a lane to a cottage. Fork right onto a path which climbs and crosses a small valley diagonally, bringing you out to a road on the hill top. The view to the west from here includes Hyde Church with its double bell tower. Turn right along the road to return to the pub.

Walk 33

The Fighting Cocks
Godshill.
Tel. Fordingbridge
(0425) 652462.

GR 176149

Mon.-Sat. 11-2.30, 6-11;
Sun. 12-2.30, 7-10.30.

P G FR Dogs welcome.
Snacks 12-1.45, 7-9.30.
Lunches only on Sundays.

The pub is named from a cockfighting pit, traces of which can still be seen across the road near the pond. Look for a neat, circular hollow a few yards across.

Walk 33

VALLEYS AND VIEWS
4 or 6 km. (2.5 or 3.5 miles.) * .
Links with Walk 34.

Both long and short walks cross the valley and involve two steep climbs. The rewards are fine views across Millersford Bottom and the Avon Valley.

From the Woodgreen Road, behind the pub, follow a bridleway. This track leads along the side of the valley, past a traditional thatched Cob Cottage. The track passes between pasture fields, giving views across the valley to Godshill Inclosure. Finally you reach open bracken covered slopes and turn left downhill, following the fence, to ford a small stream. The path climbs the opposite slope through heather, gorse and stunted pines to a gravel track at the top. The Godshill Car Park is to the left and there are fine views across the fields and moors.

The short route goes through the car park and downhill to Godshillwood Farm. A fingerpost directs you through the middle of the farmyard. Go down the track and cross the stream. There is then a short steep climb through woods to join a public right of way across fields and back to the pub.

Otherwise go through a gateway into the Inclosure and walk through a mixture of conifers and deciduous trees. The route winds downhill to a lane. Cross it and go slightly to the right up a slope. Then follow to the right of a fence to a track which is the drive to a house. Go to the right along the track just a few yards then scramble up a bank. You will find yourself on the grassy topped motte or mound of Castle Hill Fort. Go along the mound and you will find clear examples of the ditch and bank that surround this Bronze Age settlement site. Through the trees there are glimpses of the Avon valley. For better views, you need to detour north along the lane a few hundred metres. The size of the defensive earthwork is best appreciated from the lane at the north end of the Fort.

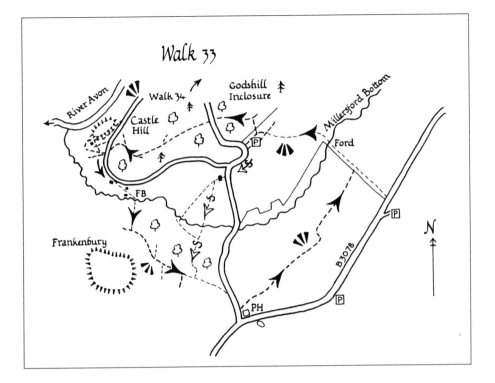

Walk 33

Return along the lane and around the bend and take the first track, past 18th century Arden Lodge and Cottage. Down beside Brook Cottage it becomes a grassy lane leading to a footbridge. A few paces along the stream bank cross a stile and go uphill across a field and then through steeper woodland, following rights of way. The rest of the walk is on the level, along a farm track and then a lovely green lane between thick hedges, to the road near the pub. From one stile on the right you can look back diagonally across the field to see the impressive embankment of Frankenbury Hillfort.

Walk 34

The Horse and Groom
Woodgreen,
Near Fordingbridge.
Tel. Downton
(0725) 20739.

GR 171176   *11-2.30, 6-11pm.*

P G Dogs welcome. Real fire.
Snacks and full meals 12-2, 7-9.30pm.

Walk 34   GODSHILL INCLOSURE AND THE AVON VALLEY
4 or 6 km. (2.5 or 3.5 miles.)
Links with Walk 33.

Go left from the pub to the next road junction. Over a stile, the path leads uphill, becoming a grassy track and then access to houses. You reach a road and ahead of you is the original Woodgreen - a lovely triangular expanse of grass, edged with thatched cottages.

If you only want a short walk then you must go to the right: either along the lanes or, for a "scenic route", follow the gravel track opposite. It leads ahead and then to the right to a group of houses. Go to the left of the houses and follow the forest boundary down, across a stream and up the other side of a small valley. At the top, you will find a small cemetery tucked away in a peaceful woodland setting on the very edge of the New Forest. A short track leads to the lane junction.

Take the Godshill road for about 250m and enter the Inclosure on the right. Follow the forest tracks to emerge opposite Castle Hill.

The longer route crosses the village green. Start along the gravel track ahead but leave it at the low "car free" barrier and head just to the right of a group of cottages to enter the forest by a gate. Leafy tracks take you through Godshill Inclosure and bring you out on the south side where there are views across Millersford Bottom to Godshill Ridge. Walk along the woodland edge to a car park and then turn in to continue along tracks within the Inclosure.

When you reach a lane, wooded Castle Hill is ahead and to the right. On the far side of it is an ancient fortified settlement site, hence the name "Castle". To visit it, the shortest route is to cross the road and go up a slope to a track. Cross that and follow to the right of a fence to the front of a house. Go to the right along a few metres of the drive and then scramble up a bank onto the top of the mound or motte. You can walk along the top of the motte, catching glimpses through

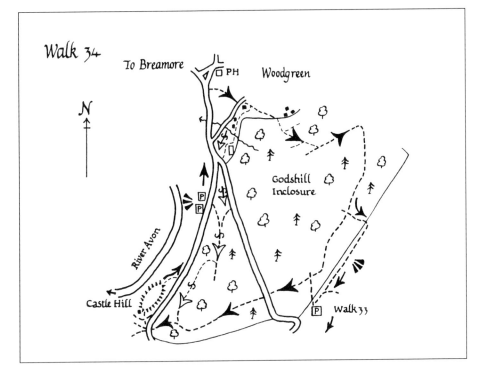

the trees of the Avon valley far below, then cross the fortifications down to the lane again.

Return along the lane to Woodgreen. On the way you will pass two parking areas where judicious pruning of the trees has opened up magnificent views over the Avon valley.

Walk 35

Royal Oak
Fritham.
Tel. Southampton
(0703) 812606.

GR 233142 *11-3, 6-11.*
Sun. 12-3, 7-10.30.

P G FR Play Area. Dogs welcome.
Snacks at lunch times.

A small thatched pub with genuine character; real fires.

Walk 35

A GUNPOWDER FACTORY
2 to 3 km. (1.5 to 2 miles.) * .
Links with Walk 36.

This short walk around Eyeworth can either start from the pub or the Eyeworth Pond Car Park.

In the valley to the west of the road a gunpowder works was set up in 1865 by Schultz. The existence of charcoal burning in the Forest attracted the industry here since charcoal was the main constituent of black gunpowder. Eyeworth is a remote area, suitable for a potentially dangerous trade. As demand increased for the more modern smokeless gunpowder, the factory grew. Three wooden huts became seventy. A weekly production of ten pounds became 15,000 pounds. The new process used imported alder wood pulp and acids. For a period there were complaints about pollution in Latchmore Brook, possibly resulting from the washing process here.

There were occasional explosions: one killed two men and maimed another. Safety precautions included the wearing of leather boots and jackets with brass buttons. Brass and zinc were the only metals allowed in. No iron was allowed, not even in the floorboards. The powder containers were zinc lined and weighed 1 cwt empty. Full ones were too heavy for horses to pull up the hill so a new gravel road was built out past the pond (through the present car park).

In the mid 1890's two shifts of 60 men were required to keep the place operating day and night. The chapel was reopened for factory staff in 1874 and some houses were built by the company in lower Fritham. A factory band even provided entertainment in the village. In 1923, the factory became part of the Nobel Combine and operations moved to Scotland. All that is left is the pond, created by damming Latchmore Brook, the new gravel road, the stables and manager's house and a few mounds.

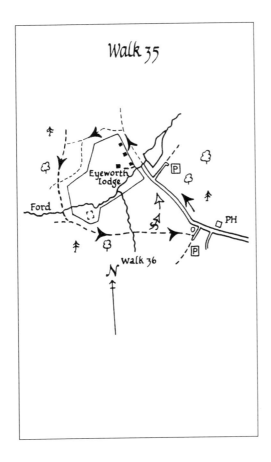

Walk 35

The walk encircles the area used by the factory, fording Latchmore Brook downstream of the site. As you leave the woods, you can see one ruined building in the field ahead, close to the stream.

If you started your walk at the pond, you can take a short cut across the grass after the track has crossed a small stream but remember to look out for the special letter box on the hill top near the entrance to the other car park. The Forestry Commission have placed an information plaque nearby to explain its history. This site saved the postman a long walk and was a safe distance from possible danger.

Walk 36   **Royal Oak** *(see page 86)*
Fritham.

Walk 36   **FOREST TREASURES**
3 or 7 km. (2 or 4.5 miles.) * .
Links with Walks 3, 4 and 35.

The long route can be walked from a number of car parks and is full of surprises: hints of the history of the Forest, distant views and fleeting glimpses of its varied wildlife.

Start at the entrance to the Forestry Commission car park. Walk through the car park where holly predominates under a canopy of oak. The woodland opens out to heather and grass with fine views. To the right is the heather clad ridge of Coopers Hill. Further to the right you can make out the traffic on the road between Brook and Godshill. Continue along this open ridge top to the second clump of holly at the side of the path. There is woodland a little to the right and, at the time of writing, a lone pine tree also on the right. A dip in the ground to your left allows a view across the valley to Holly Hatch Inclosure.

The short route turns left here infront of the holly clump and across the heather and grass. The path swings left, passing Green Pond, probably dug as a watering hole for cattle, and returns you to a lane near the old village chapel. Turn left up the lane to return to the pub.

Those with more time or energy should continue to the woods of Sloden Inclosure and keep left. This is lovely "ancient and ornamental woodland", as it is known, with a surprising number of yew trees. As you emerge from these woods there are lovely views across to the bare ridge of Ibsley Common. Cross the valley to the remote Holly Hatch Cottage. This was the home of Gilbert Smith (1906-1985), a forest keeper for many years. His book "Man of the Forest" tells of his life here. His grandfather killed the last boar in the Forest.

At any time from now on you are likely to be in the company of the shy Fallow deer. The route now gently winds along tracks up through the dark conifers of Holly Hatch Inclosure and out onto open heath again. Now you walk along a level stretch to Cadmans Pool.

At about this point, you will start to notice concrete surfaces and unnaturally straight lines in the landscape - relics of the wartime Stoney Cross Aerodrome. Your route beyond the Pool is along an old taxiway to South Bentley Car Park.

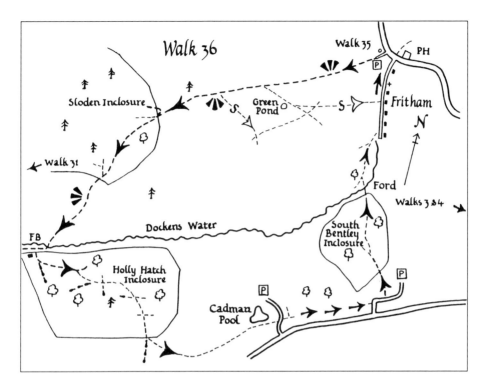

Here, turn left into South Bentley Inclosure and fork right downhill, following the edge of a conifer plantation. Go through a gate at the bottom and keep straight ahead, following a ditch to a fording point across the stream. Keep straight on, climbing very gently through Queen North Wood. The path will bring you out to a small grassy hollow. Cross this to the lane which will take you up the hill, past forest cottages and the old chapel, to the pub.

INDEX OF PUBS

THE PUBLISHERS

Ensign Publications produce a wide range of local books on Hampshire, Dorset and Sussex. We cover these three counties with town and city histories, popular local history, comparative studies in old and new photographs and with historic monographs and guidebooks and tapes. We 'live' close to our audience and pride ourselves on our ability to listen to what bookshops and their customers really want.

If you are a competent writer and have an idea for a local book, please write to us at the address below; all submissions are carefully considered. If you would like your name added to our mailing list, state your interests and the area involved and we will be pleased to send you our regional catalogues.

Ensign Publications
2 Redcar Street
Shirley
Southampton SO1 5LL

PUB WALKS IN THE NEW FOREST

We would welcome your comments and experiences on specific 'Pub Walks' to allow us to revise this book for the next edition and to plan the second volume which is already in preparation.

Each walk has been carefully planned and mapped 'on location' by the author and we have taken great care to provide clear instructions and useful information to assist the walker.

If you have particularly enjoyed a walk or a pub we would like to know. Conversely, if you have had problems with a route or if a pub has not been described accurately then please do let us know.

Please use the special Walk Report forms on pages 93-96 to record your comments.

WALK REPORT FORM

Name _

Address _

_ _ _ _ _ _ _ _ _ _ _ _ _ Post Code _ _ _ _ _ _ _ _ _ _ _

Walk Number _ _ _ _ _ _ _ _ Date of Walk _ _ _ _ _ _ _ _ _ _

Weather Conditions _

Report: _

_ _

_ _

_ _

_ _

Pub Report: _

_ _

_ _

_ _

_ _

Other Comments: _

_ _

_ _

_ _

_ _

P.T.O.

Post this form when complete to:
Ensign Publications
2 Redcar Street
Shirley
Southampton SO1 5LL

WALK REPORT FORM

Name _

Address _

_ _ _ _ _ _ _ _ _ _ _ _ _ Post Code _ _ _ _ _ _ _ _ _

Walk Number _ _ _ _ _ _ _ Date of Walk _ _ _ _ _ _ _ _

Weather Conditions _ _ _ _ _ _ _ _ _ _ _ _ _ _ _ _ _ _

Report: _

_ _

_ _

_ _

_ _

Pub Report: _

_ _

_ _

_ _

_ _

Other Comments: _

_ _

_ _

_ _

P.T.O.

Post this form when complete to:
Ensign Publications
2 Redcar Street
Shirley
Southampton SO1 5LL